HiS
PAiN
MY
GAiN

YINKA AKINTUNDE

HiS
PAiN
MY
GAiN

YINKA AKINTUNDE

RESOURCE HOUSE LTD
LONDON

First Published 2015 by

RESOURCE HOUSE LTD
resourcehouse@ymail.com
info@diademministries.org
www.diademministries.org
Tel: +44-1708 730085
United Kingdom

All Bible quotations have been taken from the New King James Version of the Bible, unless otherwise indicated in the text. 'KJV' refers to King James Version. 'Amp' refers to Amplified bible. 'NIV' refers to New International Version. 'NLT' refers to New Living Translation.

Printed for Resource House

CONTENT

Acknowledgement

To the Godhead in person of the Father, Son and the Holy Spirit, through Whom all wisdom and inspiration flow be all glory and thanksgiving.

My precious wife and lovely kids, Diadem Church members, Dele Popoola, 'Tunde Fayombo and every other person and institution who have been a blessing to my person and ministry over time.
God bless you all.

Introduction

The saying of *'no pain no gain'* is not far from the truth when it comes to the interface of exchanges that happened between a saved person and the saviour Jesus Christ. The fall of man in Eden introduced mankind to untoward pains once the spiritual death and the attending curses started taking their tolls on humanity-spirit soul and body. Everything a believer will gain in God as benefit is rooted in the finished work of redemption paid for in full by Christ Jesus on earth: in death and burial, in resurrection and enthronement.

It is my assignment in this book to show you the pain of the master so that you don't suffer needlessly again. It is also pertinent for me to show you the gains you are sharing with the master as well, you being a joint heir in his victory.

It is my prayer that the Holy Spirit will flood you up with light within as you read, to the end that you might make maximum gains in the market place of life on the account of him who loves you, and did all that could and needed to be done on your behalf once and for all to release you into unlimited gainful living.

We shall hereby trace the travails and triumphs of Jesus the Christ from the garden of Gethsemane where he started his groaning towards death, to the right hand of majesty on high where he is sitting right now.

Unto him who is able to do for you beyond my asking, even Jesus the risen lamb, I commend you now and for ever more.

Amen.

1

Crisis of Wills

The greatest gift of liberty given to mankind after creation in the beginning to determine his destiny and the turn of events therein is 'the will'. God refused to make a zombie out of mankind; He rather gave mankind the free will to choose even though he showed man what the right choice was.

God told Adam's household in Eden to not eat the fruit from the tree of knowledge of good and evil by choice in order to perpetuate the light of life called into existence at the beginning of the re-creation for all the inhabitants of the earth. Choosing otherwise would mean death, with darkness given a new foothold again on earth. Adam and his household representing mankind at large did choose the wrong side of the divide and we all know the rest of the story. Gen.3:1-24.

It is just for God and fair to all creation for God to allow personal will to play a major role in determining the destiny of whoever there is who is seeking God. Lucifer was not sent out of the presence of God and became what is known as the devil today because of adultery or fornication. Lucifer's undoing was the compromise of 'his will' with iniquity. Once his free will was compromised in his heart, it was game up for him among the angels of light in the realm of heaven. Isaiah 14:12-16.

Even when the will of God is good and perfect and chosen for you in eternity by providence as it was for Jacob before he was even born, you still need to willingly *will* it yourself to make it a reality. In grace and mercy, God will help you to *will* and do of his good pleasure but God will not *will* the goodwill in proxy on your behalf.

The Compromised Will

The strength and importance of will is clearly painted in a common saying that, "one can force a horse to the river but one cannot force it to drink from the river". It is so true in describing the weight attached to the will that has been given to us in determining our destiny on earth and even in eternity. The crisis of will became increasingly pronounced in succeeding generations after Adam up till date. The war between goodwill and bad-will, to kill or spare alive is a continuous war in every natural man. The war of will between God and Baal, God and mammon were common wars of will in the Old Testament. The wars of where to pitch one's will between the flesh and the spirit, between the World and Zion were also emphasised in the New Testament.

The Lord described the thoughts in the heart of a natural man, which is just a fountain from the throne of his *will*, as continuously evil beyond comprehension. The increasing spate of hatred and evil doings among mankind, in spite of civilization, in-spite of various rigorous measures we have developed to rein in sanity and yet to little or no avail, is a testimony to the level of corruption in natural man's will. To put it clear and simple, every natural will is compromised when it comes to pleasing God. Religion cannot cure the will of man. Paul was a religious zealot who would kill for his belief without a blink of sympathy. The same Paul had this to say regarding his compromised will just like it is in any other natural man. *"The Good I will want to do, I could not but the evil I wouldn't want to do I find myself doing".* Romans 7:13-24.

God's Will Is Goodwill

God is a constant, with him there is no variableness or shadow of turning. God's will is good all the way even after the will of man was compromised with sin. God is the only one who does or permits all things, good or evil, with good will. Once the signature of God is in it, it is good, no matter how horrible and bad it seems at first. The reason is because; in God is light and no iota of darkness at all. The will of God for mankind and his people in particular is good will to the end that he might do them good in their latter end. When you are going through tunnels and fire of life, it is easy to question God's good will and doubt his intention even though you have heard and read from the bible that they are goodwill.

Going back to the beginning, the will of God is clearly shown in the re-creation of the earth with the creation of man and the commissioning of his will. For the five days of execution of divine will, the undisputed verdict was that everything created was good. It went a notch up on the sixth day when it was declared that what was created, even mankind, was very good. Once it was discovered that the good in Adam will be compromised if he was left alone by himself, a help-meet was also found for him to keep everything good and very good. At that point onward the will of God was rested and the will of man took over. But the last that was known of God's will before he rested on the seventh day was that it was good and very good. All over the scriptures, even when God's people sin and he judged their sin with all manners of affliction, at the end of the day God will always retreat back to his original will towards man which is the good will. One of such occasion was vivid in the book of Jeremiah 29:11. Israel was in serious rebellion here and God had determined to bring them back to their senses through great trials and tribulations. In the midst of it all, God said he knew the thoughts or the will he still willed for his people which was of good and not of evil. We then need to ask why God bothers about sin. Well, God gets tough with his people when it comes to sin so that the devil will not have a foothold in their lives. Satan is the father of all sins and the force behind every compromised will which he uses to get a foothold in the lives of God's people in order to kill steal and destroy them away from the goodwill of their holy God. Thank God that even in condemning sins, His ultimate plan has ever been how to work out His goodwill for His people still.

Help Has Come For Your Will

To show the seriousness of mankind willing God's kind of goodwill, God said it doesn't matter how messed up you have been, all He wants is for you to surrender your will to His own goodwill and everything will be alright.

> *Come, let's talk this over, says the Lord; no matter how deep the stain of your sins, I can take it out and make you as clean as freshly fallen snow. Even if you are stained as red as crimson, I can make you white as wool! If you will only let me help you, if you will only obey, then I will make you rich! But if you keep on turning your backs and refusing to listen to me, you will be killed by your enemies; I, the Lord, have spoken. Isaiah 1:18-20 (New Living Translation).*

The King James Version of the bible described the "letting God help you" in the above passage as *"willing and obedient"*. The need to be helped by God in willing the goodwill of heaven was what led us to a place called Gethsemane with Jesus. The pangs of birthing redemption and the pain of emancipation started many hours before Jesus was arrested at all. The pangs took hold of the Lord long before Judas brought the pain of betrayal and the soldiers ever laid their murderous hands on the saviour.

The pain that birthed the gaining back of our will was

borne in the place of agonizing prayer by Jesus, called Gethsemane.

There in Gethsemane it was, when the issue of loneliness began. It was there that even the mere presence of Peter James and John could not help Christ in making the biggest decision in the history of mankind. A time will come in your life when all the counselling and support in this whole wide world will not suffix to help you fix your dilemma. A time when the bulk is squarely on your table and the decision is strictly yours to make. Such time was what heaven had in perspective before sending Jesus ahead to Gethsemane on your behalf. It was in Gethsemane that the conflict of interest in human will was resolved finally. It was there that the Lord Jesus broke the hold of compromise on the will of mankind in willing the goodwill of God. The transaction of Gethsemane was neither for babes nor even for lily-livered men. Even men with boldness and of strong will like Peter could not but doze off in Gethsemane of life, in the face of conflict of wills.

It was in Gethsemane Jesus offered prayers with tears and strong crying to him who was able to save him from death, even God. It was there he was heard because he feared. *Hebrews 5:6-8.* But in reality Jesus did it for your sake. He didn't need to die if not for our transgression in the first place. *Isaiah 53:6.* Jesus had to compromise his own will for the father's good will by submitting himself to the death process in that garden that night. Once Jesus said *"not my will but your will be done,"* the process of de-compromising human will was triggered and started in earnest.

It was in that garden we lost rebellion and evil will that we were bearing out of compromise in first Adam at last. It was also in that *garden of wills*, called Gethsemane, that the power of confusion lost its grip on all believers. Now we can *'will'* God's good will, we can henceforth chose aright and follow the right path in life. We now have a platform to resolve our *'will'* conflict and get back on track whenever our will runs contrary to God's will. We now have the ability and enabling power to refuse the will of Satan and his agents and stop their plots in its track. Now we can say yes to God's will.

Every Part Is Willing

A believer is no more in that position of the common saying that *"the spirit is willing but it's difficult for the flesh"*. The dominant entity in us now is the willing spirit given to us through Christ. Now we can boldly say that it is God that helps us to henceforth will and do his good pleasure. Philippians 2:13.

The pain of Christ in Gethsemane is the price tag with which we have now gained mastery over our will in willing and doing the will of God for our good. Mark14:32-41. Anything that wants to take us away from the goodwill of God is anti-Christ.

Whether we are approached through subtlety of religion or by force of attacks from any hell quarter, a believer in Christ must resist any thief coming to steal kill or destroy his goodwill in Christ. There are many manipulators out there who the bible said will creep into the flock to steal the will of people. These are evil workers to whom you must not yield for once. God's will is goodwill all the way even when the circumstance you are going through doesn't look or say so. Hold on to the will of God in faith. Christ did not just suffer for you to gain back the goodwill; he did suffer so that the goodwill of God might be done in your life.

I pray to God for you now in the words of Christ, *"Thy kingdom come and thine will be done on earth as it is in heaven"*. Since the kingdom has come into you through new birth by the faith of Christ, now may his will be fully done in your life also.

Hardship of Sweat Broken

After the fall in Eden, a significant part of the judgement of God on mankind was the curse of sweat. Sweat producing hardship, full of effort in making the ends meet till the body is worn out and drops by death. A significant progress was made in our material emancipation in Gethsemane when the Lord Jesus sweated it all out for us. More of this shall be discussed in details in the latter part of the book but bear it in mind now that Jesus Christ sweated it out for you already.

Energise Your Will in Confession

Our state of helplessness has been undone by Christ and now we are in the position of strength. Having the strength of the Lord credited to our account through Christ Jesus is one thing, making good use of it is another. One significant way to do it is by confessing through our mouth what has been deposited in our hearts. Jesus did same over and over before he eventually went to Gethsemane. No wonder he won the battle of will even though it was tough. Religion scares people with the will of God, painting a monster of will that no one can conform with. Below is what Jesus said on your behalf:

> *Therefore, when he came into the world, he said sacrifice and offering you did not desire, but a body you have prepared for me. In burnt offerings and sacrifices for sin you had no pleasure. Then I said, behold, I have come in the volume of the book it is written of me, to do your will Oh God... Hebrews 10:5-7.*

Henceforth, start copying Jesus, keep confessing and releasing your energy to conform to the goodwill of God for your life. The will of God for every one of his children, as we have seen, is good; it makes no difference therefore how it looks or appears initially. Energise your will with confession of your faith; Jesus 'said' before he did, you need to keep saying too so you can be able to do.

Let's confess together now, and keep this confession handy when faced with crisis of will as well as the other confessions in the remaining chapters of the book.

Confession of your gain over will:

I am born of God through the precious sacrifice of Jesus Christ

My former heart of stone had been exchanged for a heart

of flesh

I now do the will of God from my inside with joy as an obedient child of God which I am

Christ had fought and won the battle of will on my behalf

I am now willing and obedient unto all pleasing in everything

I therefore eat the good of the land by Christ Jesus

I am no more in dilemma regarding the will of God for my life

I am able to know and follow the will of God

My knowing and following capacity in the will of God has been activated and enhanced through the finished work of Christ

The hold of confusion and rebellion had been broken off my heart

I have overcome all crisis of will through my Lord and saviour, Jesus Christ

God now works in me both to DO and to WILL according to His own good pleasure for my life.

2

CAIAPHAS'
Court

The moment Jesus won the battle of wills in Gethsemane, his arrest followed and he was led straight to the court of Caiaphas the high priest of his day. Caiaphas represented the highest religious authority of the day. Vested on him by the virtue of his office, was the authority to act as the spokesman of heaven on earth in certain capacity. He was the visible institution who ought to have represented the invisible throne of grace here on earth. Caiaphas' office was a divinely ordained one, but occupied by a man who was only close to the institution but far from the initiator and owner of the institution. Caiaphas was he that, by position, represented a God whose will and way he knew not. He would do anything, like any other religious zealot to protect the religious institution, even at the expense of divine will and ways.

Religion Can Work Evil

Religion can make people wise like serpent but won't make them as gentle as dove like Jesus admonished, causing them to be lethally injurious. Caiaphas didn't allow Christ to be brought to his own house directly but into the house of his father in-law. Although Jesus appeared in his father in-law's house, it was on Caiaphas instructions that he was brought. Everything that happened there took place on someone else's territory which Caiaphas planned to reduce the burden of proof of his bitterness and envy towards Jesus. John18:13-14.

Do not be surprised that once you win the battle of wills by choosing the goodwill of God and begin to enjoy it, the first and fiercest battle you will confront is religion. Religion here ranges from your own and other people's religious mind-set. Religious individuals or even institutions will make your attack their calling and business above every other thing. They, like Caiaphas, are as wise as serpent but not as gentle as dove. They are out to bite and maim your person if you refuse to bow to their warped interpretations of divine will. Here are some of the evils religion has perfected.

(1) Religion Loves Shadow

The first weapon in the hand of religion is to exalt the form of godliness than the real power made available in God. Religion believes God can do all things but is quickly angered whenever God does something significant for or through someone else outside the rituals of religiosity. Religion is quick to equate suffering and lack to godliness as long as the priests are not the one at the receiving end. Religion prefers people to seek solution to daily needs from science and every other quarter except from God. The reason being simply that religion is not really interested in God's works aside the praise of men that comes with the office.

One of the major problem the Caiaphas' company of priests had with Jesus was the healing of the sick and working of miracles. They initially denied the existence of such thing as miracle. When the proofs were too overwhelming, they resorted to character assassination, accusing Christ of using demons to cast out demons. Once that did not work well, the best option left for them was to kill the miracle worker himself by whichever means. Religion will rather you suffer the pain of sickness than to seek healing in God. It will rather you come to the breath-taking cathedra built with lots of money "humbly" with no money in your own pocket. It will simply want to kill the miracle working power of God in your life.

(ii)   Religion Is Lethargic

The second evil work of religion is to mask envy and jealousy in the cloak of fighting for God. Religion is insecure; it is always threatened by truth that sets people free in Christ. The joy and exhilarating lives of Jesus' followers with the large followership courted the envy of the priests, Caiaphas in particular. Religion therefore uses false humility, false desire for holiness and false desire to go to heaven to fight true believers who have decided to follow after true godliness which is profitable in the life that we live now and the one to come afterwards. 1Timothy 4:7-10.

The profiting in the life of truly godly people cannot but stir up envy. When a religious mind makes progress, it is always premised on the pride of self-righteousness. The religious will quickly call the success and progress a product of divine reward for good deeds. Meanwhile, when true believers make progress, the religious person will then remember that all is worldly and vain.

(iii)   Religion is Judgemental

The third evil work of religion is to judge; judgement based on ignorance and false accusations with unequal scales and measures. When a religious mind sins – *"God will understand and forgive"*- they say. If someone else falls into sin, a religious man is quick to condemn and call down fire and judgement of God on such. Unequal scales and measures is the order of the day in the judgement of the religious.

Stoning the adulteress to death, while the fellow adulterer walked free is not strange to religion. All along while the priests and their companies came to Jesus' crusades to watch him preach or ask questions, it was to the end that they may judge him and not to any other genuine good intent. Religion will sit atop one thing they perceive you said and did wrong while overlooking the other one million you did well and said right.

It was against this background that Jesus was brought to the court of Caiaphas, to be condemned and destroyed because of his choice of the goodwill of God for himself and mankind in general. Suffice to say is that religion works with and for the devil most times than with and for God. Religion will rather agree with the secular unbelieving world to crucify fellow believers in God if only to make a doctrinal point or showcase piety.

Religion Bears False Witness

Another major ministry of and weapon in the hand of

religion is the use of false witnesses. The first thing the high priest and his company of religious institutions sought once Jesus was brought to court were false witnesses. Religion thrives on the back of false witnesses. It bears false witness about God and his truth. It also bears false witness against followers of truth. Matthew 26:57-61.

(i) Religion Bears False Witness about God

Misrepresentation of God as false witness of divinity is one of the major works of religion. God is often portrayed by religion as one sadist who is constantly angry and ready to pounce on "us filthy creature" without any mercy. The other side to this false representation is to paint God as not caring enough to judge or be bothered on how we live our lives on earth, whether rightly or wrongly. It muddles up the equilibrium of God's mercy and judgement to either scare people away from God or make them licentious to their own peril. It will also call evil works and attacks of the devil as acts of God so that man does not put up the appropriate resistance to such evil. It will call the deliverance and the blessings of God the work of the devil simply because it does not agree with the vessel and or method in use.

(ii)   Religion Bears False Witness about You

The accusations of Jesus wanting to destroy God's temple in the above passage was typical of religion. They are specialists in taking believers' words and faith actions out of context and giving it a bad name in order to destroy the faith. It is common for such to call our desire to indeed be the light and salt of the earth, which Jesus called us, as attention seeking and materialistic. Being earthly blessed, successful and relevant is not the same as a mere quest for earthly riches at the expense of being heavenly minded. Religion will rather so summarily judge your efforts to be the best you can be here on earth.

Generalized condemnation of all healing and miracle crusades and outreaches as mere ploy to fleece people of material contributions is a cheap campaign by religion to falsely accuse great works of ministries here on earth. It is not uncommon for religion to dissuade the healed out of the healing faith till the healing-receiving faith is compromised or defeated and sickness comes back. They go to any length to attack faith preachers and teachers with false witness. To them, telling lies based on hearsay against the people of God is just fine, as long as it will discredit the charismatic faith and paint the preacher bad.

Religion will even give you a false witness of you to you.

It will paint you as everything else but what God says you are in Christ. It will paint an unworthy, perpetual sinner of you who needs to sneak to God's presence looking down and condemned. It will tell you to walk through the market place of life humiliated, looking downward in false humility and uncertainty with your shoulders dropped like a beaten one. These false witnesses are those who make some believers think that their righteousness is still like filthy rags.

Whereas self-righteousness which we dropped at salvation was like filthy rags, we now have on us the righteousness of Christ bestowed by grace through faith! We are not some mere weak creatures barely making it through life again. We are royalty with priesthood lineage. We are identified, as saints, with the blessing and blessed all over the scripture. Religion would rather the bible wasn't written that way, it would rather we admit to and wallow in weakness and failure in the name of humility. It is such false witness that religion thrives on.

The good news is this, on that day in Caiaphas' court; Jesus took all the *false accusations* and bore the brunt therein for us, so that we don't need to bear them again. He became the victim of false witnesses and accusations so that we can gain mastery and control over the false witnessing and accusations of religion. Never again! This must be your reaction, whenever religion wants to misrepresent God, His truth or yourself in Christ to you.

Agony of Denial

It was in Caiaphas' court that the great denial of Christ by Peter, much talked about, took place. The religious company, helped by the devil, pushed Peter unto and beyond his breaking point and then the rooster crowed. Well, as agonising as the denial was, Peter recovered and got better for it. The fall of Peter and his eventual emergence painted the true picture of Christ's eternal commitment to our triumph no matter how low and down we find ourselves at any point on the journey.

Jesus, by the power of the spirit had earlier rescued Peter though prayer from the plan of the devil who had planned to destroy him and strip him of his faith substance. Jesus said Satan wanted to beat Peter off his faith substance, but thank God for our great intercessor. Luke 22:31-32. We have been declared the winner in every conflict of life before we approach the ring or even take a single punch. The devil and his company of accusers always show up late, being *'more than conqueror'* means it's too late for us to lose out no matter what we are going through right now.

Peter wasn't and didn't represent cowardice on this fateful day, mind you. He at least went far and probably further than everyone but John the beloved, as their master was being humiliated. The reality is that it takes more than strong self-will to survive the *'Caiaphas court of life'*. Peter had good motive and determination not to deny his master but by *flesh* shall no man prevail. 1Samuel 2:9c. Peter had good intentions and loved his master but it will take more than innocence to prevail in the Caiaphas court of life. The court of Caiaphas is where the insufficiencies of all that is human in the face of life's conflicts were exposed in Peter. This is where supernatural divine help is needed or else failure becomes the default and permanent feature of Christ follower.

Thanks be to God that the Lion of the tribe of Judah has prevailed in all such courts of life on your behalf. May I also say that the court of Caiaphas is where average and hypocrisy thrive pretty well. That is where people always refuse to stand and be counted for fear of failing, being misunderstood or judged. Many people were there that night too who might have benefitted from Jesus' ministry and affirmed his divinity based on proofs seen before. Many who sang hosanna earlier on in the week would have blended well with the crowd that they could not even be scrutinized or put on the spot as Peter was. Average is not fanatical about anything and so is outstanding at nothing. For fear of failure, average fails.

Religion Can Be Violent and Vicious

Religion and violence cannot be separated like night and day. Violent oppositions to the truth and violent arguments to muffle the truth belong to religion. If everything else fails, violent physical attack of the truth and its followers is a convenient path. For religion, stoning another human to death is not out of place; slitting of another human throat is allowed in religion as long as it's done in God's name. Religion is not out to save anyone, it is out to take people's will, subjugate their choice and destroy them if they show the least of resistance to any of the above .Religion preaches peace but fuels violence. That is why we tell whoever cares to listen that Christianity is the life of God given to us to live by the faith of Christ, through the power of the Holy Ghost. It is not a mere religion.

As soon as Jesus refused to conform to Caiaphas' questioning, a slap landed on his face from a zealot. Do not be dismayed at the level of violence you may experience from religious zealots simply because you have decided to see life from Christ's perspective. Slamming, slandering or slapping is religion at its best. The good news is that no amount of religious violence can stop the preaching of the gospel of our Lord and Saviour, Jesus Christ. Religion summarizes all truth under blasphemy. It prefers lame lies that can't lift the lives of the followers an inch to the truth that brings out the priest and kings in believers as God's princes and princesses. Religion did its worst in Caiaphas' court but only helped Christ towards his glorious destination. Rejoice saints, every religious attack and judgement can only bring us closer to our desired haven. You have gained ground against religion and its attending evil through the pain of Christ from same. Romans 8:31-39.

Confession of your gain over religion:

There is now no more condemnation for me because I am in Christ Jesus

My judgement is with my God according to the multitude of his mercy

I fear not what man can do to me

I am free from impure religion of man and its perverse judgements

I am judged by the law of liberty in Christ Jesus

I live to please God rather than men

I walk in love towards God and mankind

I am justified by the faith of Christ

I am free of guilt, I am free of offence.

3

Court of Pilate

R eligion can be and is, most often than not, a borrowed tool in the hands of the devil to attack faith. The world system, unlike religion, is Satan's personal property and tool and he deploys it whichever way he wants to attack the believing ones.

To validate its attack on faith, religion sometimes seeks backing from the world as well to do heinous deeds against the believing ones. The truth is that it is mostly difficult for the world to summon courage of attacking the body of Christ except they find an ally within the Church to leverage on. The allies could range from disgruntled backsliders to bitter 'had-been' who are seeking their pound of flesh by all means. People and ministries who had been at the cutting edge of God's move earlier but had lost out to distractions often make themselves available to the world as windows through which the world attacks the thriving Church. It is common to hear a former this or that calling for the world to scrutinise, tax or sanction the church. The reality is that, no genuine part of the body of Christ should be afraid of scrutiny, as we are of light, but vicious one-sided scrutiny is injustice at its best.

The last few decades have seen the profile of the Church and its capacities rose especially in the area of building financially viable organisation unlike the poverty that used to be commonplace. In as much as I will admit that no revival comes without its down side, the prosperity move inclusive, it is a shame nevertheless to hear religious people calling on the government to start taxing Church simply because the Church appears to be financially rich. If the same call has been made about other "faith groups", it could have been seen as a fair game but it has never been.

Most agitators of this are Christians so called. They are bitter about the financial prosperity of the Church and will rather be in the enemy's camp therefore. Whilst it is admitted that some financial gimmicks and indiscipline in many Christian denominations are detestable, nonetheless, nothing will make a true believer join the world system to fight the body he or she is a part of.

Some so called watch dog groups of recent went as far as scooping shredded and discarded documents from the rubbish bin of a ministry to gather facts in persecuting such ministry. What a shame! What would make a focused saint ministry stoop that low in witch-hunting another ministry in the name of fighting for the truth? Nothing should make a saint bitter to the point of forming camaraderie with the world system to attack the brotherhood of saints.

The above narrations was the exact betrayal of brotherhood Jesus experienced as Caiaphas and the religious institutions (Priestly Temple and Sanhedrin Synagogue) whisked him away to the gentile court of Pilate to be judged. John 18:28-40.

The world's Judgement

Do not expect a fair judgement on your faith walk from the world system; you are at variance with the world. Pilate was not so much interested in the doctrine, faith, mission or God of Jesus Christ or his accusers as it were. Pilate's main concern was how to prevent uproar and maintain the fragile peace in the politically tense environment he was governing at that material time. Pilate was only interested in political correctness that will at least placate the Jewish religious leaders so that they can keep their followers in check against what may trouble his government and cause him career troubles as a viceroy. He was more interested in what report would get to Caesar whom he was representing and answerable to than some religious debate about God and the Law of Moses. Pilate was a man looking for political survival with all the attending trappings of office. His judgement and outlook of life was therefore far from being wholesome.

In your walk of faith, you will be brought to the court of Pilate for judgement, this might be in your school, career or society at large. Do not feel overtly bad when they can't see life through your prism and call you unpleasant names. The fact that you don't do all the so called "cool stuff" they do doesn't make you a weak person. Hear the words of Jesus your master:

> *My kingdom is not of this world. If my kingdom were of this world, my servants would fight, so that I should not be delivered to the Jews; but now my kingdom is not from here. John 18:36*

That fact that you are different from the world doesn't make you weak; it just makes you unique. Do not let the world force you into being what you are not. Don't let it force you to be scheming and slimy, as it is, in order to rise up the career ladder. Do not let the world force you into breaking your home and violate God's ordinances about marriage in the name of gender war. You are unique and you are on a mission, the world is going nowhere; do not follow her.

Most of what the world exalt as virtues are abomination unto the Lord; it therefore cannot have the final say or suggestion in your affair. The fact that a popular celebrity by the world's standard endorses something, an idea or a way of life does not mean you have to embrace it and join in the dance. Behind Pilate's bold face as he questioned Jesus was a confused man who was in dilemma as to what the truth was, but he had to put up an act. A celebrity may be presented by the world system and the press as having it all well in life; neither envy nor want to be him or her. Behind the glitz and glamour, most time, is an empty grave full of stink and dryness beyond imagination.

The world cannot see what we see and so cannot receive what we receive; the prince of this world had blinded the world system from the right judgement. 2 Corinthians 4:3-4.How can a blind world judge a seeing saint aright? One of the biggest challenges of Christianity today is when the Church is avoiding the judgement of the world and so rather conforms. Politically correct Christianity is like Jesus avoiding the court of Pilate on his way to the cross so as to avoid being judged wrongly. At that material time while the whole court of Pilate was judging Jesus as felon that needed to be done away with, the whole angelic realm in the court of heaven were rejoicing and hailing him as the king of kings and Lord of Lords who well pleased God the father.

The World's Scrutiny

At best, the world knows you are heaven bound. In order to make your mission a mission impossible, you will be scrutinised. It is common to hear things like *"and you call yourself a Christian"*. It is part of the scrutiny. They know they are not in, but they are uncomfortable to believe that you are in either. Your words and actions will be scrutinised, the habitual liar in the world will scrutinise your words if there is a little exaggeration in it. They are not after the virtue of truth, all is about scrutiny. They will scrutinise your claim of supernatural experience till you crack and start doubting the existence of same if care is not taken. Jesus was examined, but let us see what the bible said concerning him at the point of scrutiny:

> *I urge you in the sight of God who gives life to all things, and before Christ Jesus who witnessed the good confession before Pontius Pilate... 1 Timothy 6:13.*

In the face of the worst scrutiny by the world, do not shy away from what you believe, keep saying it.

I believe Jesus is the way, the truth and the life. I believe the bible is the inspired word of God and it is profitable unto all things. I believe that my faith in Christ overcomes the world of sin, sickness, poverty, defeat and all evils. Do not delete your profession of faith on social media because of scrutiny. Do not shy away from the marriage of one man and one woman as seen in Eden because of the world's scrutiny. Preceding the passage above is one of the most profound admonitions for us as Christian:

> *Fight the good fight of faith, lay hold on eternal life, to which you were also called and have confessed the good confession in the presence of many witnesses... 1 Timothy 6:12.*

Fight the world system from silencing you through her biased and unfair scrutiny. Fight against her cloning itself into you and blurring the line of demarcation between light and darkness. Jesus had pioneered our victory over the world's scrutiny in the court of Pilate. Walk tall in the same victory of the Lord. The world must not silence you; you have gained your voice the moment the Lamb of God was led dumb to be slaughtered for you. Isaiah 53:7.

Herod's Gladness

Herod was the King of Judea that killed Jesus's cousin, John the Baptist for revenge on Herodias's behalf against his outspokenness. Mark 6:17-29.Herod was he that Jesus referred to as fox when he had earlier desired to kill Jesus not for faith matter but to assuage his fear and envy about Jesus' fame, power and influence. Luke 13:31-32.

Herod was an emotional junkie who was just interested in excitement and freaks with thrills of life as sport. He killed John the Baptist as a game in the course of such frills. Now was the time to get another dose of thrills by seeing the famed Jesus Christ of Nazareth humiliated and reduced to nothing but a common criminal in

Jerusalem. Herod was a typical pleasure seeker. Such people get excited when faith is ridiculed and saints are buffeted. When faith seems to be down and victories seem to have been lost, the Herods of this world are glad. "I said so", they easily say. They mockingly question the faith, but they deserve no answer. Luke 23:12.

The mockery of the world can never take away the victory from our faith. Jesus went through it and came out victorious on our behalf already. Nobody cares what the real name of that Herod was today, but Jesus is still very much relevant in heaven, on earth and even in hell now and for ever. Long after your mockers are gone and forgotten, your victory will still be resounding to the generations yet unborn. Every Herod's gladness in mockery is for a moment, but your own joy of triumph is eternal.

The Place Of Scourging

Even though Pilate did not find Jesus guilty of any offence according to his own words, he still could not help scourging or chastising him, which was the old Roman way of beating a criminal till the whole body is left bruised, bloodied and deeply lacerated. At this juncture, we need to re-emphasise the fact that though all of these things were being done to Jesus with the evil intentions of the perpetrators, none of these events was outside the pre-determined programme of heaven in effecting the total emancipation of mankind through the price being paid by Christ. It was not accidental, but the necessary price outlined in the book of the prophets for the final appropriation of justice to our side in favour.

> *Surely He has borne our grieves and carried our sorrows; yet we esteemed Him stricken, smitten by God, and afflicted. But He was wounded for our transgressions, he was bruised for our iniquities; the chastisement for our peace was upon Him, and by His stripes we are healed...Isaiah 53: 4-5.*

The wounding or breaking of Jesus's tissues was to pay for our breaking of God's law. His beating was for sickness not to beat us down again. The whole package of scourging was also for us to be at peace with God. Whatever challenges our guilt-free status, our health and our peace has its match and more in the price that was deposited in our account this fateful hour somewhere in Jerusalem at the court of Pilate. Peter, one of those who witnessed the scourging with a heavy heart, having just betrayed his master some few days to his graduation from being an evangelist-disciple to becoming a renowned Apostle, has much to say of what happened as

Christ Jesus was being scourged in the court of Pilate.

> *For to this you were called, because Christ also suffered for us… who Himself bore our sins in His own body on the tree, that we, having died to sins, might live for righteousness—by whose stripes you were healed. For you were like sheep going astray, but have now returned to the Shepherd and Overseer of your souls. 1 Peter 2:21-25.*

Christianity is therefore a call, a call to partake on the Lord's Table of victory. We are not called into establishing our own righteousness or paying a new price; we are only called to partake of that which the Lord Jesus has paid. The beating and lacerations of Jesus' back in Pilate's court is all we need for healing.

To an outsider, the whole business of divine healing through the name of Jesus is some scam that originated in America and amplified, like many other things, in Africa. But for us that believe in the atonement power in the wounding, bruising and death of Christ, supernatural health and healing are as real as day and night. I will like you to re-affirm your faith in the healing power through the name of Jesus Christ by his stripes and the lacerations he got in Pilate's court day and night.

When we invoke the name of Jesus against sickness, the virtues in the laceration are stirred up to our advantage. The angels of God move on the impulse of that to remove disease, repair damage and replace whatever needs replacement in our body. *Be healed of every infirmity right now, in the mighty name of Jesus Christ.*

Jesus and Barabbas

It was at Pilate's court that the first election manipulation was documented in modern democracy! Matthew 27:15-26. Same Jesus, who was being persecuted as a result of envy by religious leaders for his enormous popularity, just lost an open ballot election. Jesus who just had women and children lay their cloths and palm fronts down for his carriage to pass upon just lost an election of popularity to an insurgent called Barabbas. If the election has been between Jesus and another religious leader like Caiaphas we could rationalize the weight of followership in the equation. If the election had been a casual vote for a four year office term which shall soon come to an end, we could rationalize the political manouevre. The truth here was that Jesus just lost to a condemned offender in an election that bordered on life and death. One could feel so much disappointment until the prophetic pathway of Jesus even at his birth is re-examined again.

> *Then Simeon blessed them, and said to Mary His mother, behold, this Child is destined for the fall and rising of many in Israel, and for a sign which will be spoken against, yes, a sword will pierce through your own soul also, that the thoughts of many hearts may be revealed. Luke2:34-35.*

What an apt description of the events which just played out in Pilate's court- the hypocrisy and utter betrayal in the heart of the baying multitudes were just revealed. Same multitude that wanted to make him a king by force, whose sons and daughters he healed of diseases and delivered from demonic oppressions just voted or absconded from voting altogether. Bottom line was that the opposition just won!

Well, do not despair; it all happened for our good. This was when Jesus overcame all forms of betrayal and conspiracy with hypocrisy on our behalf. Henceforth, though they may gather but those who gather against us shall fall for our sake. The evil of conspiracy committed against Jesus became a footstool unto glory for all believers from this material time. Stop weeping because of betrayal; it cannot destroy you. It may set you back in time and material for a moment but it will ultimately set you up in destiny. Jesus suffered the utter pain of betrayal and conniving of evil men unto death for your sake; remember Judas' kiss as well.

> *But before all these, they shall lay their hands on you, and persecute you, delivering you up to the synagogues, and into prisons, being brought before kings and rulers for my name's sake. And it shall turn to you for a testimony. Luke 21; 12-13.*

Persecutions, prosecutions, attacks and betrayals are henceforth to you, platforms of testimony and turn around. Whether in your faith walk, your marriage or career, whatever conspiracy had been perfected by the scheming of men with the help of Satan will fall flat in your presence, to your testimony. The job of God's angel is to see that the elements of the New Covenant are in place and fulfilled to your advantage. Henceforth, all are to your gain and advantage.

Crown of Thorns

It was in Pilate's court that the soldiers wove the crown of thorns with which the brow of the master was bruised on your behalf. John19:1-3. With that gesture, the curse of thorns and thistles were finally broken and the crowning of mankind restored. The earth was placed under the kingship or dominion of man to yield for his good at creation; Genesis 1:27-28. After the fall of man, rebellion to yielding was infused by curse into the earth against man and to his disadvantage. The kingship and dominion of man was compromised; the earth did not have to yield according to the dictate of man any longer. His crowning became thorny, and his brow had to be tormented by thorny ground unto sweating till death. Genesis 3:17-19.

But one day in Pilate's court, Jesus brought the brow, the thorn and the sweat together face to face. There did the thorn do its worst. It didn't just bring sweat out of man's forehead; it brought blood. It saw man off to the place of death as was spoken. The thorn and thistles did the worse they could and played their part in getting justice for sin. Hence, we become free from them for ever, glory to God!

The Rod of Hardship Broken Again

The second step in breaking the rod of hardship was achieved here. The thorn had done more than God even said to the brow of mankind till mankind dropped dead in Jesus. Henceforth the earth has no right to yield thorns and thistles to a believer in Christ. *" I was there that day in Pilate's court, suffering the pains and bruises on my forehead with the master for the last time. The thorn had done its worst to me. I am done with thorns and thistles. Now I am free to prosper indeed".* This should be your disposition and confession in the face of financial challenges or material hardship.

You know Jesus said we can speak to mountains on his account. In like manner, we can speak to the earth to bring forth as we dress it. The earth in this case can be our business, career, or any legitimate means of making livelihood. It must stop yielding thorns of lack, debt and insufficiency. The crowned king in you must take charge and make gain of the crowning pain. Your crowning with thorns in Christ is the pathway to being crowned with gold. The good news is that it had been done; it's not going to be done. Your crowning with gold starts here and now unto all eternity, amen. Revelation 5:9-10.

Finally dear reader, if you are a believer in Christ with the life of God in your spirit through the redemption that is in Christ Jesus, I congratulate you. No matter how wicked or sliming the world system out there is, it cannot be to your ultimate disadvantaged again. Jesus bore all the pain of its disadvantage so that you can gain all the possible pleasures of the advantages. Jesus had this to say to you right now:

> *These things I have spoken unto you, that in me ye might have peace. In the world ye shall have tribulation: but be of good cheer; I have overcome the world. John 16:33*

Believers' battles are multifaceted in various frontiers, but when it comes to the battle against the world with all its attending challenges, do not weep, and do not wish the battle is lesser than it is. Do not even wish to die now and escape to heaven; be of good cheer. Be of good cheer not because there is no tribulation but because you are in Christ as one who had overcome. You are in victory already; the challenges met you in advantageous position of gain. You have already gained advantage against the world system because of what Jesus suffered from it on your behalf.

Good Witness Gained

The importance of having a good witness on your side is mostly appreciated in law court. It could mean the difference between losing and wining with the attending consequences. Indeed, a good witness is not only relevant in law court; it is also most desirable in the court of life. This time around, it is more than having a good witness but being one. It could mean the difference between winning and losing in life.

Not only have you been made a witness for Christ, you have also been made a witness of him. To witness for Christ is to tell what he did and who he is to mankind. To be the witness of Christ is to be the manifestation of what Christ had done and what he stands for. By your oneness with Christ through the new birth you have become not just a witness for but of him to both the visible and invisible world. When the gain of redemption is needed, you are the manifestation.

In your being the witness of Christ gain, you will face serious contradiction. The contradictions you will face witnessing for Christ are not as daunting as the ones you will face being the witness of Christ. The oppositions that will resist your preaching the gospel are not as ferocious as the ones wanting to stop you from being the gospel. What you say of the gospel is not as important to the adversary as what you become as a result of the gospel. That is why it is easier to say Jesus is a healer than being healed and remaining healthy by that same Jesus.

A Good Confession

When your experience of the gospel falls short of what you are witnessing of same, do not be discouraged; keep on a good confession as a witness of the gain in Christ. Do not tone down your witnessing confession of it. The case may look bad and against you, but what you saw as a witness is what you saw.

> **I urge you in the sight of God who gives life to all things, and before Christ Jesus who witnessed the good confession before Pontius Pilate. 1 Timothy 6:13.**

This is the concluding part of the passage of the scripture that admonished you to fight a good fight of faith. Part of the fight of faith is the *witness fight*. Keep you witness confession constant even when the circumstance looks like it has gone from bad to worse. This was the pattern of the good confession Jesus witnessed of himself before Pilate. Pilate, in the face of death for mutiny and blasphemy, asked Jesus if he was the king of Jews. Jesus did not deny it, neither did he resorted into diplomacy of say things like *"well, it is the people that said so; I didn't ask them to call me king"*. He simply asked Pilate in sarcasm: "how did you know that I am a king? Did anyone tell you or you just knew it by yourself?" John 18:33-34. This was a man facing death penalty and yet witnessing a good confession of who he was. He knew he was the king some hours ago when he rode gorgeously into Jerusalem on a colt with shout of Hosanna. He knew he was still the king now in the court of Pilate when he was being stripped naked and slapped with shout of accusations. He could not be intimidated off his confession.

You are to witness who and what Christ is to you, much also must you witness who and what you are in Christ. You are the witness of forgiveness, newness of life, healing, victory, prosperity and many more in the gain of redemption. Confess your gain as a witness when the fruits are showing, do not stop the confession when the fruits are not showing. That is how to fight a good fight of faith. That is how to be the good witness of the gain in his pain in the face of any opposition; whether the opposition is in persons or circumstances.

Confession of your gain over the world:

I am born of God
I have overcome the world and its controlling power

The greater one in me had taken the fall already

I therefore stand firm in the liberty and strength whereby Christ has made me free

I am not entangled again in the yoke of bondage

The love of the father abides in me

I therefore do not love the world, or the things of the world

I do the will of God and I abide for ever

I keep myself and the wicked ones cannot touch me

I am crucified to the world system and the world system is crucified to me

The god of this world comes and has nothing in me

I belong to God by Christ Jesus

I have overcome the world and its wickedness.

4

The Way
of
Golgotha

Crucifixion in whatever sense it is implied is no picnic. Either literal crucifixion or the implied crucifixion to self, none is pleasant to human experience. Jesus didn't pretend that going to cross was fun. He even said that going to cross was a sorrowful but inevitable thing he just had to do. Matthew 26:38. Christ having gone through that distressful way had conquered the challenges therein for us and has predetermined the outcome of whatever 'going-through' you are experiencing right now in the rough way of life.

When you read or hear a preacher sounds as I do, the first thing that may come through your mind is that we don't really know how rough your way has been or even is right now. You may even be tempted to accuse me of insensitivity, but before you close the case as thus, hear me out. The finished work of Christ which we preach and teach might not remove challenges from your path and may not reduce the intensity of the challenges you are going through. Nevertheless, the finished work of Christ will energize you to be able to bear it and not be broken by it.

Secondly, the finished work of Christ will see you through it unto the pre-determined manifestations of your already won victory which is just round the corner. 1 Corinthians 10:13. The word temptation here is same as trial or challenge or the roughness on the path of saints. You can bear all, because you have won all in Christ already; ultimately you will emerge with gains of victory.

Too Tired To Bear More

It was a real roller coaster of sort in the life of Jesus for the past twenty four hours or so. From the battle of prayer and the betrayer in Gethsemane to sleepless night with treachery and beating in Caiaphas and Pilate courts. He has been moved from prison to judgement in the most inhumane way you can imagine. He was denied a fair trial in the court of man to secure fair trial in the court of God for all humanity. Jesus was wrongly condemned to death by men through envy, but was rightly condemned to death by God through love. It was the condemnation by God on our behalf that brought atonement and justification to all through faith in him today.

With every ounce of strength he could muster, Jesus faced the very last phase of the journey of no return towards Golgotha once and for all.

It was a journey of no return because it was a terminal journey that would bring a final closing of the curtain for sin and its era of spiritual death with impunity and wickedness in the history of mankind. It was a journey of no return because the weak, stripped, condemned and battered prototype of fallen man going up the mountain for retribution would soon be no more for ever and ever.

But this man was tired. Tired was he that he no longer could bear the cross again. It was he who admonished all to carry their cross and follow him, but it was same he that couldn't bear his own any longer. A man by the name Simeon of Cyrene was compelled to bear the cross for Jesus for the rest of the journey.

Of serious importance in the transaction taking place at this material time was the fact that, every weakness and inability Jesus bore as a man in the process of redeeming us was deliberate and necessary. He literally took our place in every sense of it. If Jesus didn't go through this weakness and tiredness, the weak and the tired would have gotten no hope of victory in him today. But thanks be to the Lord that he bore the weakness and became tired so that all that come to him can be well succoured in their own day of weakness and tiredness too.

You may be so tired right now of life or any of your pursuits that giving up is the only reasonable thing you can muster. Hold on a bit, your help is on the way. Jesus has pioneered the way of gain out of all tiredness and weakness for us all. Maybe you have even given up already, you may be down and think you are out; there is much to gain for you as you leverage on the one who got tired for you that through his tiredness you might be made strong.

The place of tiredness or even falling is no more the end of game for us that believe; much more still lies ahead. Below are the words of one of us who learned to leverage on the tiredness of the master for renewal of his own depleted strength.

We are troubled on every side, yet not distressed. We are perplexed, but not in despair. Persecuted, but not forsaken. Cast down, but not destroyed. Always bearing about in the body the dying of the Lord Jesus that the life also of Jesus might be made manifest in our body. 2 Corinthians 4: 8-10.

Why would they go through so much and not yet defeated: *"because they bear the dying of the Lord"*. This is not exactly same as bearing the death. It simply implies that they put into consideration and use, the dying process underwent by Christ for them. Part of that dying process was the weakness and inability to continue the carrying of the cross. Once they put that process into the equation of their life, *"the life also of Jesus was being made manifest in their body"*. This implied that they were enlivened; they gained strength of life to continue and win unto the end. They gained strength through the dying process of the Lord. It's your turn to gain strength too. When Christ was too tired to bear it, he received help; may you receive help to succour you too in days of trouble.

Pitied for Dying

One of the words that we don't like talking about is death or dying. We are so much troubled about dying as well as the process by which it occurs. This is not peculiar to this generation but had been so for ages. This was Jesus, a thirty three year old promising young rabbi being led to a place of dying a very agonising death reserved for the accursed among men, for humanly no just reason.

There would have been protest upon protest on ground and on the internet if this happened today. No small diplomatic strain would have developed between the axis of Rome-Jerusalem and the rest of the world. But now every possible protesting voice had been either subjugated or manipulated by the religio-political institutions of the priests and Sanhedrin. All that was left were the muffed voices of pity from the sidewalks of Golgotha's highway. Some smote their breast wondering that if such could be done to a living tree, how much their leaders could do to a dry one. If Jesus with his national fame, his might and followership had suffered that level of humiliation and injustice, 'who was safe?' was definitely one of their meditations.

So they pitied him. They pitied him for not having what it could have taken to take on the power that was in his day. They pitied him that he probably over rated his own hype and now no one was there to really fight for him. They even asked why a man who opened blind eyes couldn't now save himself from this terminal humiliation and extermination. They pitied him for being a good man and yet suffering injustice. 'Life is not fair' would have been the final verdict of many as they saw the man who rode into town few days earlier on an ass with pump and pageantry then climbing the place of the skull enveloped in mortal bruises.

Some could not hold their emotions, and I wonder who could at that stage if not the murderous ones. They therefore wailed for him, they forgot that he was a Galilean, they let go of racial and tribal sentiments, Jerusalem women wept for the man who had suffered so much even though he was a Galilean. You know Jesus was not the only one to be crucified that day, there were two others but no one bothered weeping for them. Maybe because they were justly sentenced and condemned, maybe because they were certainly not as bruised and battered like Jesus Christ. For whatever reason, Jesus was the most pitied man on the street of Jerusalem that fateful Friday afternoon. But the master took the pity with candour - weep not for me but for your children who might be lost without taking the advantages and using the benefits of all these am doing, he said in essence to the wailing multitude. Luke 23:27-31.

We have passed being pitiable, we are now in the position of strength. No amount of pity is comparable in benefit to what Christ had already gone through for us that believe in him. So, whenever you are going through challenges, don't seek pity; seek the way out. In fact we are asked not to count it strange beyond imagination when we are faced with challenges. There is gain in the trial of our faith, gain beyond gold in value. Christ had already wired the gain into it for us.

Maybe you suffer injustice in the hands of men, or you feel helpless in pulling your weight, it shall still turn to you for a testimony. Jesus had gone through these pitiable states for you so that you won't be tied down there, if you ever go through those routes for any reason.

You may be experiencing a grace to grass condition now and all you can see are the good old days when you rode the colt, even the foal of an ass into town like Jesus did into Jerusalem but all you can feel now is pain and pangs. You probably can only see dimly and faintly the helpless faces of acquaintances beholding your battered state with trepidation as Jesus did on the high way of Golgotha. I have got the very good news in the good news of the gospel for you. Jesus had gone ahead of you to make a deposit against these dreadful days you are going through. He had gone ahead to turn this phase around for your eventual good. There is gain to be gained in this phase of your life, come out of self-pity and gain your gain.

Do not solicit for pity, you don't need it; all you need for the road had been deposited into your account one day on the road to Golgotha. Do not start throwing tantrum and fouling up everywhere around like a helpless one, you are not helpless. Even when those who ought to do something to help you refuse to, the gain in the wearied journey of Christ on your behalf that fateful afternoon in the desert of Palestine will compel and command the appropriate help for you. Remember that a Simeon showed up from nowhere that day to help the master. Your own God ordained help will yet show up; Simeon is in the corner right now.

When you go through any unpleasant experience in the school of destiny, believing people may even pity you for being a victim of too much believing. They pity you for being so brain washed by faith preachers and teachers. They blame you to have believed that God could do anything about your hopeless case. Be of good cheer, Christ was in your shoes for your sake, but today his triumph is undisputable. Your gains will appear to all who had pitied you in like manner.

Mocked For Dying

The dying process is one unpleasant but needful process if a seed will bring forth more according to its destiny and inherent capacity for fruitfulness. In the same way, for Christ to fulfil his glorious destiny as a redeemer and bring many sons as himself to God, death was a must. It takes real trust in God who revitalizes the dead for one to submit oneself to the process of dying. There is no real trust that has no verbal expression. Jesus had been expressing his trust in such God over a period of time and had been misunderstood for that same reason.

Jesus had been having his say of faith for a long time to the angst of mockers. The only problem was that they had not been given the golden opportunity to see him fail, fall or falter and so their cynicism had no wind under its wing for flight. The way to Golgotha was the day they had been waiting for and now was their long awaited opportunity to call his trust in God what they really thought it was, delusion.

The mockers were allowed by heaven to have their free day; they stripped him of his cloth and mocked him. They had no respect for his dignity as a human talk less of as a servant of God. The more they thought God would intervene and there seemed to be no intervention, the more their theory of him as an impostor got vindicated. They teased him with king's robe of purple and crown of affliction and got away with it scot free. They spat on him and yet heaven didn't fall. What other evidence did they need to prove that the man before them was just another want-to-be impostor who was just calling himself what he really was not in the name of God?

When the dying process sets in any area of your life, I promise you that the visage might be marred than you could have envisaged. The pain and the accompanying tiredness become more overwhelming than what you planned for. It is at that particular time the mockers will extract their own pound of flesh. You will be misquoted, maligned and ridiculed beyond your wildest imagination. The mere fact that you are going through tough times despite your belief in victory and dominion through the finished work of Christ is what cynics need to give credence to their theology of suffering and failure. People who are going nowhere need to see a man on full speed to experience a little halt for them to justify stagnation. Mockers will assume that they are on heaven's side because it looks like God is not intervening or even there at all in your time of challenges. They will love to strip you of your robe of dignity and put on you what they deem fit. They will spit bad words on your person and add salt to the injury to drive home the point that you are just an ordinary man or woman who had been under illusion of being special all this while.

Do not despair my friend, Jesus went through that route ahead of you, not only to set an example but to disarm the power of mockery on your behalf. The shame of mockery didn't take anything from the destiny of Jesus but complemented it and made it speak out loud and clear. In like manner, the mockery and shame of the now has no permanent resting place in your destiny. Christ went through it in order to make you immune from it; it can only end up for you one way and that way is the way of glory.

You need to treat it the same way Jesus did. How did Jesus treat mockery or shame? He despised it. To despise means to demean it. He made it of no value and weightless in his value system. You have to stop paying attention and giving weight to mockery and cynicism. You have being wired and positioned to make nothingness of such. It has no effect any more on your journey and takes no value from your destiny. It can neither stop you nor mar you again; it can only multiply your harvest.

> *For your shame ye shall have double; and for*
> *confusion they shall rejoice in their portion:*
> *therefore in their land they shall possess the*
> *double: everlasting joy shall be unto them.*
> *Isaiah 61:7.*

The whole chapter of the book from which the verse above was taking was talking of the destiny of saints who will live in the Church days. The rest of the chapter are our present realities after the first group of verses has already been fulfilled as Christ said in the temple when he was asked to read. Luke 4:16-21. Henceforth, the least return in glory for every shame is double. Your confusion will be turned around and your double portion of glory will come. You will possess your goods back in double and your joy shall last for ever.

I still have a word for you:

> *Therefore then, since we are surrounded by*
> *so great a cloud of witnesses [who have borne*
> *testimony to the Truth], let us strip off and*
> *throw aside every encumbrance*
> *(unnecessary weight) and that sin which so*

readily (deftly and cleverly) clings to and entangles us, and let us run with patient endurance and steady and active persistence the appointed course of the race that is set before us. Looking away [from all that will distract] to Jesus, Who is the Leader and the Source of our faith [giving the first incentive for our belief] and is also it's Finisher [bringing it to maturity and perfection]. He, for the joy [of obtaining the prize] that was set before Him, endured the cross, despising and ignoring the shame, and is now seated at the right hand of the throne of God. Just think of Him who endured from sinners such grievous opposition and bitter hostility against Himself [reckon up and consider it all in comparison with your trials], so that you may not grow weary or exhausted, losing heart and relaxing and fainting in your minds. Hebrews 12:1-3.

Confession of your gain over tiredness, pity and mockery:

Thank you Jesus for suffering the pain of tiredness on my

behalf

I have gained strength to run the race of life in you

I am not fainting, I am not falling and I am not faltering

Thank you Lord for looking pitiable on my behalf on your way to Calvary

Now I have gained mastery over pity

I am not a victim, I am victorious

I am not to be pitied; I am to be envied by the world

I am not into self-pity; I am a king on the earth, decked in glory of victories

Thank You Lord Jesus for taking all my shame and mockery away

Instead of shame, I have double glory

I am not faint hearted; I am not losing heart

I am going all the way for glory; In Jesus precious name.

5

The Place of The Skull

I n the eye of God, there is only one judgement for sin, and that is death. God said to the first Adam in Eden that the only judgement for breaking the law given him will be death. All other effects were just side effects of the spiritual death; every evil on earth today is a side effect of sin and death. Sin has only one direct effect which is death. Since the only judgement meet for sin is death, if anyone therefore will take the judgement on behalf of mankind, such one must pay the penalty with a sinless life.

Divine Judgement

The only one who can count sin or could be sinned against is God and so He is the only one who can and is allowed to judge sin. Governments can mete out punishment to serve as deterrent for breaking the law of the land. Romans 13:1-5. Churches can discipline members for not doing the right thing so that such errant one can be remorseful, repent of evil and come back to the way of truth and life. 2 Corinthians 5:8. In all of these, the power to punish sin is still of God. We are not endowed to determine or punish sin on God's behalf, simply because the concept of what sin is did not originate from man in the first place. It was God who called sin what he wanted it called and measured out the right punishment for it in and from the beginning of creation.

The punishment God measured out for sin is death, spiritual death or separation from the life of God which was followed by and manifested as all other accompanying deaths. Being the God-man he was, Jesus had been carrying the life and presence of God as his life until the time of judgement came. At that material time, God departed and death was measured out to Jesus as mere-man representing the whole family of mankind. Sin was fully and finally judged and retributed in man for ever.

Shedding of Blood

If dying alone was all that was needed for the full wage of sin and its effects to be paid for, Jesus could have just slept and not wake up (die) or poisoned on our behalf. If Jesus had died a bloodless death, the judgement for sin would have been meted out but the remission or erasing of sin would have be missing in the process. Sin was a wrong that had to be judged; it was also a monster that had to be remitted. Sin was a wickedness that had to be destroyed, not just an error that could be pardoned. Sin was an accusation that must be overcome and not just a wrong doing to be judged. We gained back good conscience towards God and man in the remission of sin by the shedding of the blood of Jesus, the lamb.

Pierced All Over

The sensual veil of flesh had been the greatest instrument of sin and inlet window for Satan to get a foothold on human affairs since the fall. It had been the hindrance for the manifestation of the treasure in the human spirit for a long time. This stronghold of flesh was broken in all possible ways as Christ was pierced in all possible places of significance on our behalf.

You see my dear friend, Jesus could have died any way

and anyhow if all that was significant to God in redemption was just the price for sin to be paid. As far as God was concerned, the concept of sin and redemption is beyond mere shedding of blood and forgiveness. God knew the significance of the fall and the attending curses, struggles and metamorphosis it brought along with it. Apart from the piercing of Jesus' brow with the crown of thorns which we saw earlier as the second break in the hold of hardship; of significance it is for us to see the three other violent piercing Jesus underwent for you, especially at the Calvary hill.

(i)   Pierced in the Hands – The hanging of Jesus on the cross is not just for death; he could have been killed in any other thousand ways. The hanging on the cross was to the effect that the curse of life will be lifted off us permanently. The curse at Eden on Adam was the mother of all other curses that could ever be. That was the curse that made any other curse possible and of possible effect on any mankind. Ranging from the curse of Balaam which represented *diabolical curse, to the curse of Mosaic Law, lineage curse and even the curse of cause-and-effects.* The presence of curse was leveraged once there was a lifting of the blessing at the fall in Eden. For the blessing to eventually come and stay as God planned it and spoke to Abraham and the fathers, the curse had to be permanently broken. It was the hanging of Christ on the cross that got the job done.

> *Christ has redeemed us from the curse of the law, having become a curse for us for it is written cursed is everyone who hangs on a tree that the blessing of Abraham might come upon the Gentiles in Christ Jesus. Galatians 3:13-14a.*

One significant place of operation of curses of life is in the hand of man which is the organ of tilling and the channel of earning and productivity. Ability to till the ground is not as important as the ability to receive back your input in commensurate harvest. When curse is at work, much effort will always yield less fruits and much frustration. Much frustration may lead to much health challenges till the body cannot take it any longer and drops. Jesus broke this evil curse the day his hands were pierced. The curse of non-productive effort was pierced, and now you can go and bring forth in abundance as God intended for you in all your career endeavours. The earth received blood from the hands of Jesus as a witness that your case is different when it comes to tilling and yielding. You have gained profiting by blessing.

(ii)   Pierced in the Feet – Jesus was not nailed in the feet in order to just attain a balance of his weight on the Calvary tree. Even if that was the wisdom of the Roman soldiers, more was in the mind of the father. The connection between man and the earth which was to yield him fruits are his two feet. In Adam, God cursed the ground for man sake: in Jesus the curse was broken as the connection was pierced. Every time man walked the earth until that fateful day on Calvary, there was always a witness and remembrance of the curse. A reminder that the best of fruits, minerals and other resources locked up within the earth had been given the permission to become a snare of thorn and thistles once harvested by man. No wonder mankind live in a world so rich in resources, yet rife in poverty.

For you a believer in the finished work of Christ, the story has changed. Walk the earth with the expectation of milk and honey. Work on the same and expect the fats thereof to flow your way. The curse connection has been pierced through the master's two feet. The earth received the blood from Jesus' two feet as a witness that your case is now an exception from the curse as you walk about the land of your occupation.

Above all, Jesus was bruise (pierced) in the feet so that the head of the serpent, even Satan, who is mankind's eternal enemy may be bruised. Man fell in Eden when friendship was developed through subtlety between man and the serpent (Satan). God in His wisdom said the way back up for man is the way of enmity between man and the serpent. A bitter enmity that will lead to bruising on both sides of the divide till man has the eternal victory. Here we see Jesus bruised on his feet on his way to bruising Satan on the head through death. On that fateful day, once the feet of the woman's seed (Jesus) was nailed, a chain reaction was set off which culminated in him destroying Satan on our behalf through death once and for all. Genesis 3: 14-15. God's judgement on Satan was triggered on our behalf once the feet were pierced. Now we can say boldly that the prince of this world has been judged and cast down for us. Now have we been granted power to thread upon snakes and scorpions and everything that represents the power of the enemy by gain in Christ's pain.

(iii) Pierced on the side – In Deuteronomy 30:19, when God wanted to show his people how life and death with the attending blessing and curse operate, he called heaven and the earth to witness. The connection between mankind and the earth or ground when it comes to the manifestations of the blessing and curse was also clearly spelt out in the whole chapter. This explains the need for the piercing of Jesus' side as accounted in the Bible.

> *But one of the soldiers with a spear pierced his side, and forthwith came there out blood and water. John 19:34.*

Same way heaven and earth was called to witness the matter of life and death, of blessing and cursing against God's people in rebellion in the Old Testament, heaven and earth was called into witness here at Calvary that obedience has been accomplished by mankind.

In the beginning, the three personalities of God had it on record that man was a blessed being created to enjoy the fat of the earth. They also bore record to the fall of man from this great place of blessing through disobedience in Adam.

> *For there are three that bear record in heaven, the Father, the Word, and the Holy Ghost: and these three are one. 1 John 5:7.*

More significantly was the need for an earthly record of witness that the price of fall was paid and the curse was put paid to. Henceforth the blessing might eternally flow in man's direction.

> *And there are three that bear witness in earth, the Spirit, and the water, and the blood: and these three agree in one. 1 John 5:8.*

The spirit of Christ departed his body down to the place of the dead beneath the earth; his water and blood came out upon the ground to complete the witness in earth that 'the curse is over'.

> *For whatsoever is born of God overcomes the world: and this is the victory that overcomes the world, even our faith. Who is he that overcomes the world, but he that believeth that Jesus is the Son of God? This is he that came by water and blood, even Jesus Christ; not by water only, but by water and blood. And it is the Spirit that bears witness, because the Spirit is truth. For there are three that bear record in heaven, the Father, the Word, and the Holy Ghost: and these three are one. And there are three that bear witness in earth, the Spirit, and the water, and the blood: and these three agree in one. If we receive the witness of men, the witness of God is greater: for this is the witness of God which he hath testified of his Son. 1John5: 4-9.*

Your triumph over the curse of want and lack of productivity with its accompanying poverty is rooted in your faith in the pierced Jesus. Heaven and earth have the record that he was pierced all over for your sake that you might not harvest thorns and thistles on earth again. The curse of life has been totally and eternally destroyed for you. All that is now left behind on earth for you is the blessing that compels your harvest of milk and honey with the fats of whatever ground of your occupation.

Power of Satan Broken

There is nothing as heart breaking as to be in a situation where you don't have a say in what and who has the power of control over your life and affairs. This is why coming unto Christ involves a *conscious decision of making him the Lord over your life.* At this point, you are appropriating something significant in the work of redemption. Of significance is to know that at the fall, the authority over whatever was on earth, mankind included, was transferred from Adam to Satan. Do you mean the power over Adam was in Adam's hand at Eden? You ask. The answer was absolute yes. That was why He (Adam) and not God or anyone else was the determinant of the eating the fruit in the midst of the garden or otherwise. This was part of the *'all this power'* Satan said he was given while tempting Jesus in Luke 4:6.

At the cross Jesus gained back this power in similar fashion Adam lost it. How did Adam lose the power? You may ask. The answer was *through disobedience of God's command.* When God was disobeyed in Eden, Satan was given the control. Now at Calvary, God was obeyed and so Satan was dethroned from his stolen throne and the stolen power taken back from him.

Fear of losing out, if that means disobeying God, was the key through which Satan tricked the first Adam out of power. Genesis 3:5. Not minding to lose out, if that means obeying God, was the key Jesus used to gain back power and break the rulership of Satan over human affairs. Philippians 2:6-11.

You have gained the mastery over your life back in Christ Jesus. Satan is no more in charge. Stop sounding like the devil has an overriding power to do and make you do things outside your will. Stop fearing that the enemy can just do as he wishes with you, your destiny or any part of you, spirit soul and body. The overriding power over your life is now back in God's camp through Jesus Christ. Philippians 2:13. You gained back the control room of life and its overriding power at Calvary.

Power Of Death Regained, Fear Of Death Destroyed

Physical death has various agents including sickness and many other attacks. Every agent of death has one face deployed ahead to prepare the ground of man's life for attack. His name is called *'fear'*. Fear is more than being just afraid; it is a state of having lost the duel before the bout. It is a state of no need for resistance or putting up a fight as mere formality; a state where you see every effort from your side as inadequate to meet up with the perceived ability of your assailant.

Jesus saw death and all its ugly errand agents as prey he could defeat and free mankind from once and for all. This he surely did and handed us the most needed victory over death which starts with victory over the fear of death. Hebrews 2:13-15. The power of death which was stolen from Adam had been in abuse by the devil until Jesus showed up on the scene.

Death itself needs its numerous agents to attack the body to a state of it not being able to bear human spirit any longer before it strikes. Think of these agents in their worst form as mere errand boys of death and treat them in boldness as such. Whether it is diseases, sickness or any other attack; you have gained mastery over them when you were liberated from the fear of their master through the death of Jesus Christ at Calvary.

The Accuser's Mouth Stopped

The worst punishment anyone can take for offence in any land and under any judicial system is the death sentence. Capital punishment is the harshest and non-lenient sentence anyone can get. To underscore the significance, room for appeal is always opened for the condemned at least for judicial conscience sake. In our case, our sacrificial lamb refused to press for appeal when he was offered by Pontus Pilate. Having been charged and placed on the line for capital punishment, Pilate pressed upon Jesus to appeal his case but Jesus wanted the accuser to enjoy the momentary victory by declining any appeal. He totally yielded himself to their accusations and died the death. Not even some scourging or beating from Pilate would make Jesus appeal his accusation. Mark 15: 3-5. He took all of the accusations and shut the mouth of the accuser once and for ever. You forever have gained mastery over the accusation of Satan and his entire host on earth or beneath the earth that moment Jesus' blood was shed at Calvary based on false accusation.

> *And they overcame him by the blood of the Lamb and by the word of their testimony, and they did not love their lives to the death. Revelation 12:11*

No More Records

Of major note among what took place at Calvary was the wiping off of records.

> *Blotting out the handwriting of ordinances that was against us, which was contrary to us, and took it out of the way, nailing it to his cross. Colossians 2:14.*

Why was Jesus so particular about certain records that he had to take them along to the cross at Calvary to make sure that they were wiped off there? The above passage said the reason was because those records were contrary to you. They were written to work against you. Such records probably even preceded your existence on earth. They may be literally written down or have been covenants made in your lineage, or curses incurred by your ancestors. The good news is that Jesus took them along to the cross and wiped them clean with his blood. They could be records before God or records with man or Satan, what qualifies them for wiping is *whether they are for you or contrary against you.* Once any is contrary to your wellbeing, the eraser or wiper on the cross is activated for clean wiping process till nothing stands contrary against you again. The stubborn ones amongst them that would have wanted to stand on your path of progress were *'taken out of the way'.* You need to see them taken, nevertheless, for them to stop harassing and speaking against you as if they are still valid. They could be genetic codes written in your flesh or blood, thereby causing health problems. It is time to agree with the new record which says they had been taken out of your way.

Nothing ought to be standing as barrier on your path again. Any roadblock, now that you are saved, is illegally mounted and must be dismantled by light. Nothing has the legal right of standing in your way to good life and godliness gain. Jesus left no stone untouched in the work of redemption. He knew the kind of culture and family you would be born into before he embarked on the Calvary journey for you. He knew that being born into certain families might give certain forces of darkness the legal right of road block on your path and so he made the above bailout provision in your second birth.

Jesus didn't just wipe the hand writings and their accompanying road blocks against you, for example marital spells, premature death or any kind of lineage misfortune. He took them out of your way and nailed them to His cross. Whatever remains today as manifestation is a deception from the enemy to keep you bound and in that former position of perpetual disadvantage. This you have to stand against and fight as a soldier with the power of truth from your gained position of victory.

God Pleased and Pacified Forever

Conflict between man and God can only end up in one way and one only. All the governments of this world with their wealth and other resources at their disposal cannot prosecute a successful war against God. It is a dangerous thing to be in conflict with God. It is better not to be born than to come into this world and leave without making peace with God. God had conflict with mankind at Eden because of disobedience. At Calvary, God's anger and wrath was permanently pacified. One major work of redemption Jesus did was to broker and seal peace between man and God. Man was declared never guilty (justified) and fit to be at peace with God thenceforth.

> *Therefore, having been justified by faith, we have peace with God through our Lord Jesus Christ. Romans 5:1.*

The notion that God is still angry and mad with us is of the devil and a significant deception at hardening man against taking steps at reconciling whatever is wayward in him with the perfect will of God.

You have gained peace with God, He is not mad with you anymore and that is even before you did one single good deed after salvation. Your position of actions now is as of one pleasing God and configured to please Him as your default. God's presence departed Jesus Christ, the God-Man on the cross, to signify the ultimate manifestation of God's displeasure with man in his sin-carrying state. Jesus lamented this departure with great lamentation before he gave up the ghost and died as if he were God-less. But thank God that peace was brokered for man at that moment of Christ's death; the wrath of heaven was pacified with divine presence restored for ever.

Confession of your gain at Calvary:

Thank you Jesus for taking the fall for me on the cross

I celebrate your death in Calvary as my initiation back to life

Your death is my entrance back into life

You were pierced in crucifixion that I might be blessed

Your hand was pierced that the curse might be taken from my labour

Your feet were pierced that my walking the earth might be curse-free

Your pierced side bore witness to my freedom from the curse of death

I have gained the power to live and prosper in the works of my hand

Every barrier has been taken off my path

I am free from the fear of death and Satan

I am at peace with Jehovah God, through Christ Jesus my Lord.

6
Selpulchre
of the Rich

K indly note that all that Jesus Christ did and was either as a teacher, a prophet or 'God-man' up to the point of activating the process of our redemption at Gethsemane, he had done without our involvement. But onward from Gethsemane when he yielded himself totally to the will of God the father to kick-start the redemption process for mankind, we were there all along and all the way in him. We were not there with and in him when he opened Bathemeus eyes or raised Lazarus from the dead, but we were in him when he was beaten and crucified. Everyone who will ever be saved in Jesus Christ till the final day of judgement was inside and with the man Jesus all the way through his suffering and unto his triumph from the garden to the throne. We were in him as he was caught in the dilemma of yielding or struggling with his will relative to the father's will in the garden. We were with him as he was being betrayed by the friendly kiss of a protégé called Judas. We were in the man Jesus as he was being falsely accused by the high priest and judged by Pilate. We were with him as he was beaten, scourged, mocked, stripped, humiliated and dragged on Jerusalem's blood stained high street to Golgotha. We were with Jesus on the cross as he finally took the pain and agony of death and gave up the ghost.

Buried in Baptism

Know you not, that so many of us as were baptized into Jesus Christ were baptized into his death? Therefore we are buried with him by baptism into death: that like as Christ was raised up from the dead by the glory of the Father, even so we also should walk in newness of life. For if we have been planted together in the likeness of his death, we shall be also in the likeness of his resurrection. Knowing this, that our old man is crucified with him, that the body of sin might be destroyed. Romans 6:3-6.

The above scripture shows us what transpired and our inclusion in the whole of that fateful weekend; from his arrest on Thursday evening after the Gethsemane experience to Friday afternoon when he was buried. We were buried with Christ to fulfil what was written concerning man that after physical death, ashes and dust should go to where they all came from. The end of all living is when the spirit departs the body *(death)* to go and meet God for judgement and the body is buried or subjected to disintegration of sort back to where it comes from which is the earth. Ecclesiastes 12:7.

Significant to note in the burial of Jesus is the sixth verse of the scripture above. Our old man was buried with Jesus and totally destroyed at this point. The old man exited the equation at this point and remains buried for life. No matter how much we cherish departed loved ones, all we could do with them ends when the earth receives the body. At that point, what remain are only memories and deeds done before death and burial. In like manner, our old man ceases existence and stops being the centre of activities and attention in our life. What keeps many in wrong doings are memories of habits and deeds not properly deleted and dealt with.

The man or woman born into so or such family with so or such dysfunctionality had been buried. He or she had ceased to exist in the reckoning of heaven and has to be reckoned as such in your consciousness here on earth or else the power of hell will keep taking advantage of the lack of synchronicity between your reality in heaven and on the earth. The power of your burial with Christ will find full expression in your life when you start divorcing your earthly experience from your eternal reality. What I mean is that you stop equating what you feel or what is going on in your life, no matter how tangible and visible they are, to the true state of thing in your redemption status.

What is going on in your life will soon be displaced by what ought to be when you insist on what ought to be because you know and won't take it otherwise. The old is buried and gone and if for any reason it wants to rear its head with the help of Satan and fleshly environment, you must submerge it again and again till it stays buried.

Did We Just Lose Out?

Have you ever wondered the level of expectation in the heart of the disciples of Jesus from the point when he was arrested to when he died, as if the master would do something? Even Judas thought Jesus would do something. They all knew how powerful he was and they had seen him dealt with all kinds of gale forces in the past, so that would not be an exemption to the master's retinue of victories. But to their utter dismay, not only did Jesus die, he was seen being prepared for burial and off he went into sepulchre.

The news was that God-man unto whom the voice came from glory that he was God's beloved in whom heaven was well pleased has died on earth. Not only was he humiliated and killed, he was now being buried like any other ordinary mere mortal beneath the earth. Oh, the palpable trepidation, angst and searching of hearts amongst his followers. Remember they all left their life-long careers to follow Jesus. Some of them had probably sold their equipment and de-register from the union or association that had been regulating their trade.

Did we just lose out? Were we deceived to have believed that he was really what we thought he was? So deep was the damage of doubt the sealing of the grave, with Jesus inside, did to their mind that brother Thomas made up his mind and choose a new believe system forthwith. 'Henceforth I won't believe anything again till I see and feel it', he had said.

Maybe you had hoped, believed, prayed and did all that needed be done and was almost certain of the victory only for failure and defeat to just stare you square in the face. My friend, do not despair; it is only just a burial. With your God, burial is never the end of the matter. It may appear like we just lost, but it can never be for long. Our affliction, no matter how heavy, is made light with us knowing that it is just but for a moment. The set back is for a moment, the lack of reckoning is just for a moment.

Much Going on Behind the Scene

The place of the dead is a quiet place. Everyone must have consoled as much as they could and then their mouths were sealed and the talks had all gone. Outside Jesus' grave were guards watching for any activity of sort so they could fix, as men trained to fix situations. On their activities log book from Friday afternoon till Sunday morning could have been boldly written 'nothing eventful' and 'no activity'.

Whereas it looked like there were no activities going on in the outside, much was going on in that grave and in the place of the dead. Spoiling of principalities and powers was seriously taking place. Colossians 2:15. Jesus' mortal body was being ministered to and overshadowed by the power and glory of the father. Romans 6:4. The Holy Ghost was midwifing the greatest miracle in the history of mankind, and yet it looked like nothing was going on in the outside.

Maybe your life looks like nothing is really going on and yet you have prayed, fasted, given and did all you can. I have a word for you, my friend. You are being prepared behind the scene and curtain of flesh for a miracle. It's quiet and lonely in the outside, oh dear soldier, but much is going on within that grave. People may be mocking you while others may be wondering what has become of your faith; but much beyond what the mortal eyes can see are taking place to your advantage.

Resurrection was an event that took place on Sunday morning, but behind it were processes that took two nights and days. God is working on your case, the process might not be eventful in the outside as you wish, but the result will be glorious like the resurrection morning when it manifests. The oppositions are being disarmed; you are being readied for eternal newness of experience. Not until the soldiers were knocked off into coma kind of sleep and stone rolled away for the master to come out, did the kingdom of men know that our God works behind the scene indeed, no matter who is watching. Mathew 28:2-4. It's been quiet for long, but be ready now for your earth-quaking miracle. It won't be long again and you shall see your change come.

Qualified For Fresh Start

> *Therefore we are buried with him by baptism into death: that like as Christ was raised up from the dead by the glory of the Father, even so we also should walk in newness of life. Romans 6:4.*

Every born again child of God is qualified for a fresh start no matter how bad and wrong things could have gone. We cannot stay down for too long, our affliction must only be momentary. Rest has been worked into our schedules of destiny. A Christian life must not just be a cascade of struggles and challenges without victories. You have been qualified for rest. You were buried so that God and his angels can work while you rest and wake up to reap the spoils of the victory of the Lord while it is God's turn to rest.

You Belong Up Here

Burial for you, as was for Jesus, is a transit; it is your registration for greatness and far reaching connections.

> *And he made his grave with the wicked and with the rich in his death. Isaiah 53:9a.*

What you need to realise with the burial moments of your life is that God wants to expand your reach and horizon. God wants to increase your relevance; he doesn't want you to be boxed up in a small click of socio-economic or other strata. Jesus came as the saviour of the 'whole world' and not a small segment of society. He came to save the ones like you and the ones unlike you. For this cause, he has to fill all to save all.

> *Wherefore he saith, when he ascended up on high, he led captivity captive, and gave gifts unto men. Now that he ascended, what is it but that he also descended first into the lower parts of the earth? He that descended is the same also that ascended up far above all heavens, that he might fill all things. Ephesians 4:8-10.*

The descending moments of life must give you hope rather than depress you. They must be the prophecies and pointers to the plan of God for your life that exaltation is on the way. You belong up here, which is why you descended down there; that also like your master, you may fill all to help all and save all. Those who belong up here don't usually start up here; they start down there and ascend up here.

No matter how deep you have been buried and low you have gone; one of the major gains of being buried with Christ is the gain of ascension. You shall soon gain height.

Confession of Your Gain in Burial with Christ

Thank you father God for the low moments of life

I recognise that as Christ was buried in the lower belly of the earth

So have I been buried with him in Baptism

I fear no descent or low moment again

For every descending is to launch me up in higher ascension

Every low moment is to take me higher and further

The graves of life have no power over my destiny again

Holding forces have being spoilt on my behalf.

Nothing is holding me back again

Nothing is holding me down again

In Jesus precious name

7

Ascended
Lord

nd ye are complete in him, which is the head of all principality and power, in whom also ye are circumcised with the circumcision made without hands, in putting off the body of the sins of the flesh by the circumcision of Christ. Buried with him in baptism, wherein also ye are raised with him through the faith of the operation of God, who hath raised him from the dead. Colossians 2:10-12.

Every pointer in prophecies and diagnosis of man's state in the original and fallen state shows that man belongs at the up. David being in the spirit heard a conversation made towards God by another being as recorded in the eighth chapter of the book of Psalms. In the conversation, a question of admiration was asked of what man was that God was mindful of him and visited him. The next observation was that the man was made just a 'little lower' than the angels. Psalms 8:4-5. The next verse showed that the 'little lower' state was a temporary state. It was so, because afterward, every work of God's hand was then placed under man's dominion and every other creatures was placed under his feet. It takes real height for all things to be under you.

In spite of the *Elohim* content of the above scripture, the bible in context still shows us that God made man a little lower than 'the angel' and not a little lower than God himself. The writer of the New Testament book of Hebrews definitely read the original manuscript of the Old Testament and not the English version where many told us that the word Elohim was translated as angels because of the awe of God. The book of Hebrew's writer was inspired by the Holy Ghost to quote this same Psalm 8:4 verbatim while comparing mankind in Jesus to angels, and not to Godhead. He also gave the reason for the term 'lower than'.

> *But one in a certain place testified, saying, what is man, that thou art mindful of him? or the son of man that thou visits him? Thou made him a little lower than the angels; thou crowned him with glory and honour, and didst set him over the works of thy hands. Thou hast put all things in subjection under his feet. For in that he put all in subjection under him, he left nothing that is not put under him. But now we see not yet all things put under him. But we see Jesus, who was made a little lower than the angels for the suffering of death, crowned with glory and honour; that he by the grace of God should taste death for every man. Hebrews 2:6-9.*

Death as far as we were concerned in Christ was a matter of mere tasting. Jesus 'tasted' death on your behalf. What this means is that the downstream of things depicted by death, for you, is a momentary experience. Some are dead, some will die, but we tasted death. It was not and can never be our permanent state of existence. We were made a little lower than we should be in God for a moment and now restored back to our new estate in the risen Lord and saviour, Christ Jesus.

All are said to have sinned and fallen short of the glory of God. Redemption for us therefore means we have come up from the fall and risen up from short. We are now risen up never to fall or be made short again.

Risen For Our Justification

We were tricked into the fall; God in his mercy had judged us guiltless once the ultimate price of death was paid on our behalf for the fall. Resurrection is to prove our *'non guilty'* status. Jesus could have died and just gone to paradise and then heaven via the realm of the dead like Abraham or Lazarus did without physically resurrecting. But he had to physically resurrect and prove to the whole creation that man is now just and has a *'never guilty'* verdict on him now in the court of heaven.

We are not just an old self picked up and dusted but rather a new brand from the womb of redemption. We are like 'never existed before breed'; we have no record of guilt or conviction kept somewhere against us anymore. Through resurrection of Christ, you have gained *'not guilty'* status.

He Who Is From Above

We need to understand the origin of our specie in Christ Jesus. As natural men and women in the image of the first Adam, we were a people of the earth from the earth. Having been re-born in the last Adam, the origin of our specie is now above.

> *The first man is of the earth is earthly; the second man is the Lord from heaven. As is the earthy, such are they also that are earthy: and as is the heavenly, such are they also that are heavenly. And as we have borne the image of the earthy, we shall also bear the image of the heavenly. 1Corinthians 15:47-49.*

Resurrection brings you back to where you truly belong which is up among the stars. You were raised with the stars (heavenly bodies) in Christ Jesus. You have left the dust (earthly) because that is not your realm. You are now with the stars (heavenly) for that is where you have been transported to through your resurrection with Christ.

In this your resurrected form, don't settle for dust, do not settle for low. Aim high and go even for heights higher than the stars. Resurrection has overridden the gravity law of life, in pursuits and achievements, for you so that nothing would be potent enough to keep you down again in your entire endeavour.

The angel had strange news for those seeking Jesus in the low place of grave on the resurrection morning. 'He is no more here but risen' was the classic. No matter how low and gravely you have gone, I pray for you to exhibit the resurrection order in you right now. It is the plan of God for you to come up again, and stay risen for ever. In the resurrection of Christ, you have gained 'from-above' status and approach to life.

Not Allowed To See Corruption

> *In the sweat of thy face shalt thou eat bread, till thou return unto the ground; for out of it were thou taken: for dust thou art, and unto dust shalt thou return. Genesis 3:19.*

The corruptibility of man was heaven's verdict once the seed of sin (corruption) was sown in Eden through disobedience. But like in any case of justice and its execution, man became not only corruptible just after death but while alive. Humanity became like plant and the glory like flower and both became victim of corruption at the mercy of the corrupter, even the devil.

1Peter1:24. It is not therefore uncommon to see a once flourishing health crash suddenly and take everything a man has along with it. It became a common thing for a once peaceful and flourishing career or home to just crash to the canker of corruption. The good news is that corruptibility was taken into consideration while the new man was being conceived in the belly of death to be born through resurrection unto life in Christ.

> *Because thou wilt not leave my soul in hell, neither wilt thou suffer thine Holy One to see corruption. Thou hast made known to me the ways of life; thou shalt make me full of joy with thy countenance ... He seeing this before spoke of the resurrection of Christ, that his soul was not left in hell, neither his flesh did see corruption. This Jesus hath God raised up, whereof we all are witnesses. Acts 2:27-32.*

Here we see Jesus spared the impact of the corrupting power of hell so that you too might be spared of same in your new estate in Him. Hell, death and the grave have nothing to spoil in your life again. You have been given the life of the incorruptible last Adam. Ashes and dust have nothing to collect from you again. Not from your body, career, marriage or lineage. You are not allowed to be corrupted by the power of hell. You have had enough of your life going up and down, beautiful today and very ugly tomorrow. No more beauty and glory today but ashes tomorrow. You belong in the breed of the incorruptible by the virtue of your participation in resurrection. If you are born again; you were dead, buried and now risen with the Lord in the ever enduring form of glory.

> *Being born again, not of corruptible seed, but of incorruptible, by the word of God, which lives and abides for ever. 1 Peter 1:23.*

Through the resurrection of Christ, you have gained an enduring wave of glory.

Risen But Better

Resurrection is not just an event, it is also a pattern. A pattern your life must assume; a pattern your faith must enforce. It is a pattern the wisdom of God in you must see and embrace as your expectation and way of life.

> *So also is the resurrection of the dead. It is sown in corruption; it is raised in incorruption. It is sown in dishonour; it is raised in glory: it is sown in weakness; it is raised in power. 1 Corinthians 15:42-43.*

This is the pattern God intends your transition of life to take when you come into Christ to partake in his resurrection. Dishonour and weakness are expected to give way to glory and power. Whatever natural disadvantage you were born into and have suffered from by the reason of your natural birth has been taken care of in resurrection. Resurrection is a form of birth, a new birth into glory and power; a new birth from being just natural into being supernatural and spiritual.

True spiritualty has its anchorage on the resurrection of Christ. He opened the floodgate of life and light into the realm of the celestial for us. Now you can lay demand on the glory and power of resurrection in you to fix any form of challenge that could have brought you or any aspect of your existence into dishonour and weak position. Through the resurrection of Christ, you have gained a better platform and a better pattern of outlook of life and destiny expression.

Quickened and Transformed

In resurrection, Jesus' body experienced infusion of the life of God and transformation from mortality to immortality. The power of God and the glory of God overshadowed and worked on his body to the end that it was transformed and risen. Romans 1:4. In as much as we live in mortal bodies for a while here on earth, we must appreciate our partaking in Christ's immortality at the same time. Of note is the fact that immortality and mortality had always been in co-existence. In death, mortality had the upper hand but in resurrection immortality prevails. The good news is that, immortality has swallowed up death in victory through Jesus our risen Lord at the resurrection.

The implication is that we are no more at the mercy of mortality and all agents of death in our bodily life. On this point can we access the quickening power of God and employ same for the servicing of our mortal body while still living in it here on earth.

> *But if the Spirit of him that raised up Jesus from the dead dwells in you, he that raised up Christ from the dead shall also quicken your mortal bodies by his Spirit that dwells in you. Romans 8:11.*

If by any reason you ae experiencing set back of sicknesses and diseases in your body, even if an organ is dead or has failed; the infusion of life into and transformation of your body are parts of your gain in Christ's pain. We gained healing and prevention of sickness in our body, again through the resurrection of

Jesus.

Always on Time

One major gain of resurrection is that we are 'always on time'. No more delay in breakthrough. When God promised the children of Israel deliverance from the house of bondage under the hand of Moses, the deliverance was delayed for thirty years for one reason or the other. This amongst many other proofs made us to realise that breakthrough can be delayed. But no more delay for you; and not again in our risen Christ. When Jesus showed up on the scene, he said the whole imprisonment under the belly of the earth and the pulling down of his earthly temple (whose temple we are) will only last for three days. As it was spoken by Jesus, so was it done. At the nick of time on the third day, we rose up with the master. Our resurrection was not delayed for a second longer than was scheduled.

> *Jesus answered and said unto them, destroy this temple, and in three days I will raise it up. Then said the Jews, Forty and six years was this temple in building, and wilt thou rear it up in three days? But he spoke of the temple of his body. When therefore he was raised from the dead, his disciples*

> *remembered that he had said this unto them; and they believed the scripture, and the word which Jesus had said. John 2:19-22.*

No more delay in fulfilment of promises and prophecies, no more delay in laying hold of your desired turnaround. Isn't it funny that many Christians still believe that Satan has so much authority and power that he can just bring about delay as he likes in matters that concern them. How you feel or the history irrespective, the truth is that if Satan couldn't change the time schedule of resurrection by a second, your issue of delay is over

The Jews had documented histories of delay including using forty six years to build what Jesus said he would build figuratively in three days. All he was showing them was that the era of building in flesh and being unnecessarily delayed is now over. You have gained *'on-time'* grace by the timely resurrection of Jesus Christ our head. No more delay.

Confession of Your Gain in Resurrection

Thank you God the father

For raising me in and with Christ

I have been quickened by your life that raised Christ from the dead

I am being overshadowed by your glory every day of my life

The grave can no longer hold me or mine down

The very life of God flows through and services my life bodily here on earth

I am not where I used to be

I am now raised with stars in Christ Jesus.

8

Sitting On Throne

King of Kings

'After resurrection, what happened to Jesus Christ?' is a good question. He is alive and doing well on the throne of life in heaven where he is ruling and reigning as the Lord of Lords and King of kings! The current and eternal placement of Jesus is much and far higher than any other throne, name, power or dominion in heaven, on earth or in hell beneath. Ephesians 1:19-23. At this lofty position, nothing can challenge or escape the influence and power or authority of Jesus Christ. This is good news for us his followers. Better news is the fact that we are also included in this lifting and positioning of enthronement.

Father God in his compassion and mercy had carved out a place for us in his plan and heart of kindness with love. We too are NOW lifted and sitting in that same position of authority, power and dominion on the account of Jesus Christ our dear Lord, saviour and brother. You are therefore an enthroned being; you are settled and sitting on the throne of life. Your command centre is far higher beyond the reach of whatever force you are warring with here on earth. It is higher than ancestral and lineage forces. It is higher and greater than any flying power in the air or any marine force on the coast.

> *But God, who is rich in mercy, for his great love wherewith he loved us, Even when we were dead in sins, hath quickened us together with Christ, (by grace ye are saved;). And hath raised us up together, and made us sit together in heavenly places in Christ Jesus. That in the ages to come he might shew the exceeding riches of his grace in his kindness toward us through Christ Jesus. Ephesians 2:4-7.*

Ruling Lord

'More than conqueror' for you means you did not just

win with Christ, you are practically reigning with him. You have passed winning stage of conflict of life. You are in dominion, reigning and enjoying the fruits of the Lord's conquest. The Lord Jesus is the Lord of every Lords, physical or spiritual. The lordship of Jesus translates to the lordship of the saints. Whatever Jesus is ruling over by the power of his might, is now made subject to us.

Do not let anything, situation or personality lord it over you or your life at the expense of you enjoying whatever the Lord has won for you in victory. Capacity to refuse being lorded it over is what you have gained through your enthronement with the Lord Jesus. A Christian must therefore never feel helpless again under the burden of this world system or the operational forces thereof. You have gained lordship and mastery over every force of life as far as your destiny is concerned. You are set down on the throne of life to permit what you want and disallow what you do not want in your life.

On The Right Hand

We are sitting with Christ on the right hand of majesty on high! This does not mean that all that Christ and God had been doing since resurrection was just merely sitting literally on a chair in boredom and doing nothing. The expression is a figurative description of settlement, enthronement of Christ Jesus in the *most privileged and preferred place of authority* as it related to God the father. God is good all the way and so his literal right and left sides are good in His most holy place of abode in heaven.

> *The LORD said unto my Lord, Sit thou at my right hand, until I make thine enemies thy footstool. The LORD shall send the rod of thy strength out of Zion: rule thou in the midst of thine enemies. Psalm 110:1-2.*

The Lord Jesus had been given the preferential place and the most prestigious place in the scheme of things in heaven by God the father. He is at the right hand of the father which indicates where authority and ruler-ship flow from. This is where the word of the king proceeds from with power and nothing anywhere can withstand him. Ecclesiastes 8:4. The good news is that this is where you are sitting too. Glory to God.

You are right now, in Christ, sitting on the right hand side of privileges and preference as far as God the father is concerned. Your words are loaded with power. It makes no difference what ten thousand adversaries have spoken against you before you show up. Once you show up and declare a decree by the name of Jesus every knee must bow to your words and every tongue must be in conformity, to the glory of God the father.

Sitting on the right hand of majesty means God is now pleased with you. The right and left hand had been used figuratively to indicate being pleased with and displeasure respectively by the Lord Jesus in the bible. Matthew 25:33-46. Stop looking for alternate ways for God to be pleased with you; he is already pleased with you in Christ Jesus. All you need now is to live in accordance with his good pleasure as shown you in His word, like a favoured child which you are. You have gained privileges, preference and the pleasure of the father. Live so.

Hidden Life Is Higher Life.

> *If ye then be risen with Christ, seek those things which are above, where Christ sits on the right hand of God. Set your affection on things above, not on things on the earth. For ye are dead, and your life is hid with Christ in God. When Christ, who is our life, shall appear, then shall ye also appear with him in glory. Colossians 3:1-4.*

Unlike your unbelieving contemporaries, there is more

to you than the eye meets. People have this misconception about a saved life, thinking whatever we gain and possess here on earth as a result of the blessing of the Lord on us is our most prized possession. Not at all my friend, the most valuable part of you is not kept in any bank or behind any gated compound of this material world.

The first Adam had his life in a secured garden here on earth before he had it compromised. The last Adam has his own life hidden in God the father in heaven where robbers and moth cannot corrupt or plunder it. It is in that same *'Fatherly Bank of Heaven'* that you have your life tucked away from assault.

When you are being threatened by mere mortals whose ultimate assets and access are limited to here on earth, you need to relax and be confident of being secured based on your location in Christ. Our dear brother Stephen knew this reality so much that, even when the religious persecutors had battered his physical body with stones based on false allegation of blasphemy, he still knew his life was not in their hands. He had to beg the Lord Jesus who was holding his life to please release him so his flesh can ultimately rest in sleep. Act 7:57-60.

Whenever chaos breaks out on earth or the earthly supply is being compromised by any means, stop fretting and losing hope like the people of this world. Your place of abode is far beyond harassment and molestation by man-made or natural disaster, famine or problem. This truth has to sink down within you and so change where you set your heart and affection. This is the higher life you have gained in Christ, do not settle for or be reduced to anything lower than higher.

Higher Sight

We were admonished in Colossians 3:1-3 to set our gaze as people who live far above. It is higher sight for higher life for us. Having been raised with Christ far above, we need to start engaging our vision advantage. We are the ones who can access what natural and mind eyes have not seen. 1Corinthians 2:9-16. Your higher position is not just a privilege to be merely celebrated, it is a call to higher challenge in taking responsibility. It is a call to see into the mind of God the father in heaven while you are here on earth. A call to feed like an eagle on uncommon things in purpose and pursuit of the Father's plan for your life. You cannot just settle for what the eyes are seeing and what ears are hearing and what just crosses the mind of mere mortal. For example, marriage and relationship for a Christian cannot just be reduced to mere sensual feeling. It can neither even be a mere court endorsement of what is right nor wrong nor what the mind of a movie director put together on the screen.

Life decisions and choices for you cannot be based on mere natural senses; you are entitled to higher intelligence from heaven. You have gained height in Christ for sight in God. You are now able to see evil coming far ahead and hide yourself in the wisdom of God. Proverbs 27:12. In like manner, you can see the good ahead and position yourself for it by the wisdom of God. Your lifted position in Christ has given you foresight advantage. Just like the earthly nations of the world use satellite planted in outer space for exploits in intelligence, you have gained higher sight for exploits too by the reason of your planting in heavenly place in Christ Jesus.

Confession of Your Gain in Heavenly Places

Thank you father for lifting me with Christ into yourself

I am sitting on the throne of life in God
Far above molestations and harassments

Beyond the manipulations of darkness and its agents

I have been restored back to dominion in Christ Jesus

I dominate my aura with the light of life

I am privileged of God and favoured by men

My life and living are not of this world

I see with higher sight for higher living

My affection is set on things above

I am resurrected, rested and restored to dominion

9

Gain From Loss Concept

A s we round up the master's steps towards humanity's total redemption, we need to come to terms with the principal fact that the whole concept of redemption is a concept entrenched in losing one to gain more. The first Adam was told he would lose life (die) if he did what he was commanded not to do by God. True to the warning he did lose life. He lost life because he couldn't lose out on one thing, which is the allure of the fruit from the tree in the middle of the garden. Everyone like him lost through him and in his order.

In like manner, the Lord Jesus was promised he would gain all if he could lose one. He hence choose to lose his life (die) against the allure of staying alive and thus gained unlimited life back for himself and everyone like him and in his order.

He Lost All to Gain All

> *But we see Jesus, who was made a little lower than the angels for the suffering of death, crowned with glory and honour; that he by the grace of God should taste death for every man. For it became him, for whom are all things, and by whom are all things, in bringing many sons unto glory, to make the captain of their salvation perfect through sufferings. For both he that sanctifies and they who are sanctified are all of one: for which cause he is not ashamed to call them brethren, Saying, I will declare thy name unto my brethren, in the midst of the church will I sing praise unto thee. Hebrews 2: 9-12.*

(i) Jesus lost height that he may regain higher height on your behalf. *Hebrew 2:9*

(ii) Jesus lost his superiority over the angels for a moment, that we may gain angelic ministry through him for ever. *Hebrews 2:9.*

(iii) Jesus lost his mortal life that we may gain immortality in him. *1 Thessalonians 5:9-10.*

(iv) Jesus lost the comfort of heaven when he ventured on earth that we may gain access to the comfort of heaven on earth through him. *2 Corinthians 9:8.*

(v) Jesus lost God's company that we may gain divine company for ever. *Mathew 27:46.*

(vi) Jesus lost being the only begotten of the father that we may gain his brotherhood in the sonship of God the father. *1 Peter 1:3.*

(vii) Jesus lost his righteousness and gained sin for a moment that we may lose sin forever and gain eternal righteousness of God in him. 2 Corinthians 5:21.

(viii) Jesus lost his biological family that we may gain the family of God. *Ephesians 1:5-6.*

(ix) Jesus lost his glory and gained the shame of mockery that we may gain his eternal weight of glory. *Luke 23:35-36.*

(x) Jesus lost invincibility and gained vulnerability for a moment that we may gain power. *John 19:10-11.*

(xi) Jesus lost flesh and blood that we may gain communion of life and strength for living in his body and blood. *1 Corinthians 11:24-30.*

(xii) Jesus lost his visage to beating and battering

that we may gain healing and peace. Isaiah 53:4.

(xiii) Jesus lost joy, gained grief and was acquainted with sorrow that we may gain eternal joy unspeakable, full of glory. *Isaiah 53:3b.*

(xiv) Jesus lost his right to fair hearing and justice that we may gain justification. *Isaiah 53: 6-12.*

(xv) Jesus lost his will to please himself, that we may gain our place in God's good will and please Him. *Luke 22:41-42.*

(xvi) Jesus lost to Satan and all the powers of hell for a moment through death, that we may gain victory and mastery over Satan and all the powers of hell for ever. 1 Corinthians 2:7-8, *Revelations 1:18.*

(xvii) Jesus lost heaven's compassion in judgement under God's wrath, that we may gain mercy, compassion and favour. *Isaiah 53:10.*

(xviii) Jesus lost his voice to the worldly, religious and political mob of his days that we may gain our voice and not be subdued and swallowed up again by any opposition, no matter how loud and vicious they are today. *John 19:12-16.*

(xix) Jesus lost his clothing and dignity for a moment that we, in him, may be clothed in glory of heaven and dignified for ever. *John 19:23-24.*

(xx) Jesus lost the ambience of living in heaven to make an abode on earth for thirty three years that we may gain a place of heavenly mansion. *John 14:1-3.*

(xxi) Jesus lost his life 'as cursed' that we may gain our lives 'as blessed' through his cross. *Galatian 3:13-14.*

(xxii) Jesus lost his life under the LAW that we may gain eternal life under GRACE. *Galatians 4:4-5.*

Let Your Gains Count

Nothing is left to your disadvantage again after resurrection. The fear of losing out is rooted in self, and self is what can make the losses Christ had suffered already not to count as gain in the life of a believer.

> *And I heard a loud voice saying in heaven, now is come salvation, and strength, and the kingdom of our God, and the power of his Christ: for the accuser of our brethren is cast down, which accused them before our God*

> *day and night. And they overcame him by the blood of the Lamb and by the word of their testimony; and they loved not their lives unto the death. Revelation 12:10-11.*

As far as heaven is concerned, all the testimonies bore of Jesus in this book and many more in terms of the gains he has brought to us through salvation for our total emancipation are true. They are real, worth saying and celebrating with a loud voice. The one who will believe these testimonies or reports according to Isaiah 53:1-2 will definitely see the hand of God revealed in his or her life to enjoy such gain as he or she believes.

The other balance to the manifestations of these gains was described above as *'having not loved their life unto death'.* This simply reinforces Galatians 2:20 to the effect that you, unlike what you were in the first Adam, have overcome the fear of losing out where 'self' is rooted. Like the last Adam (Jesus) you have to let go of all to gain all in God.

I will briefly help you with the toxic self(s) you need to deal with daily for you to maximize the gain of Jesus' pain.

Flush Out The Toxic Self(s)

(i)   Self-Righteous – To be self-righteous is to give yourself a pass mark in an examination you did not conduct. It is a state of setting yourself as the yardstick of measurement when the standard is even beyond your prerogative. God is the one who sets the standard of righteousness, because righteousness is a function of how you stand with and before Him. It is a right standing before God, not before the world or yourself. Every arrival on righteousness based on how you measure up to any other standard is like filthy rag before God. To be self-righteous is to make yourself the standard rather than God. It is idolatrous. Self-righteousness will make you too filthy and not measure up for the gains of redemption. Lose self-righteousness, and gain all things that pertain to life and true godliness by Christ Jesus.

(ii)   Self-Sufficient – Self-sufficiency is excluding God's provision and promises for life and Godliness in what you need to be complete and truly satisfied with. Satisfaction outside reliance on God is self-sufficiency. Religion, material wealth, intellectual wealth and other non-material element of false-satisfaction can make one self-sufficient. Believers in Christ can also be in this sad state by simply believing that all they need God for is to forgive their sins and allow them into heaven on the last day. Every other thing in life; they, their families or government will take care of. They only believe in God because of horror of hell not that they are absolutely dependent on Him as their ultimate source. Self-sufficiency will make you too big for the gains of redemption. Lose self-sufficiency, and gain reliance with dependence on God.

(iii) Self-Centred – Every believer in Christ is just a little part of a bigger picture. A little part of a bigger picture called the Church of Christ which is even a part of the bigger picture of humanity as a whole. Whatever Christ is to you or did for you is to the end that you will be the channel of Christ; being and doing same and even more for others. The blessedness of the new creation starts when you stop living just for and unto yourself. 2 Corinthians 5: 14-15. Self-love at the expense of Christ-love is self-centeredness. It will short-circuit the gains of new creation. Life is not and cannot be all about you and your gains. Redemption has a larger picture of you being the extension of God's saving hand. Self-centeredness will make you bottle up the gains and lose them after all. Lose the self-centeredness, and gain being a blessing.

(iv) Self-Loathing – When you pay too much attention on yourself, the tendency to start loathing yourself because others around you are not paying as much attention to you as you wrongly expect is very high. You don't have to be the subject of discussion and scrutiny all the time. When your magnifying glass is always on you, very likely you will start seeing the cracks and the pebbles the casual lookers aren't seeing and slip into condemnation, self-demeaning and self-loathing. When you loath yourself, you will not see the gain you have acquired nor the progress you had already made in Christ. It will still be about what is missing and messy according to your friend's and society's standards. You will start making it look like Christ forgot to cover some grounds for you in the work of redemption. At best, you will blame yourself for it all; instead of praising God for paying it all and congratulating yourself for gaining it all. Self-loathing will make you disqualify yourself from the gains. Lose self-loathing, and gain glorious living in the image of Christ. Be grateful.

(v) Self-Pitying – Simply put, to self-pity is to perfect the art of being the victim. Victim of Adamic fall and a dysfunctional background. Victim of a cruel world and a powerful devil. Victim of bad church organization and an unconcerned God. Self-pity is an unclean indulgence like any other. It gratifies the emotion and locks the champion within you in prison. Self-pity makes people subconsciously work towards loss and defeat in order to justify their never good enough position on things and outlook of life. They are always the victims, the wronged and the disadvantaged. Whereas, as a believer in Christ, all things are now yours. You are now in the vantage position of life, go and gain it all. Self-pitying will make you overlook and underrate your gains. Lose self-pitying, and gain victorious living as a redeemed of the Lord.

Confession of Your Gain from Loss

Thank you Jesus, for losing all that I may gain all

I have lost my filthy garment of self-righteousness

I have gained the righteousness of God in Christ

I have lost my pain and sorrow

I have gained health in Christ and joy of the Lord

I have lost my shame to gain the glory of heaven

I am free from self and have gained the Lord.

GAIN

5 6 7

3 8

2 9

1 0 10

10

Make The Gain Count

C hrist's work of redemption is heaven's ultimate investment in humanity. For every investment, a measure of profit is expected. God wants you to be profitable to His kingdom, for yourself and humanity as a whole. You are chosen as a stock worth heaven's investing upon; you cannot but make it count, that which Christ had done for you.

Make It Count For Heaven

The ultimate gain for the kingdom of heaven is that the conflict between man and God is over. We, who were enemies by the separation in our hearts from God, are now heaven's friend and treasure. Heaven can now count on you for sweet savour of worship. You can now shine the light of heaven on earth through good works that men on earth may see and glorify your father who is in heaven which they cannot see.

It glorifies and gladdens Jesus when, through him, you come to and know the father intimately. It makes the travail of his soul on your behalf worth it. Eternal life is when you come to the full knowledge of God the father through Jesus Christ his son, and this is the ultimate gain there is. John17:3.

You are the staying hand of heaven against the unleashing of evil from the kingdom of darkness on earth. You are heaven's mouth piece to judge evil. You cannot sit on the fence when it comes to good and evil. Mathew 5:13-14. It therefore glorifies God the father, when through you every knee is bowing to the Lordship of Jesus in dominion, figurative or literal.

You are heaven's answer to mankind's prayer on earth; a channel of manifestation of the resurrection power. The signpost of the hope of God's calling for all humanity. You are the access to the riches of heaven's inheritance for mankind to enjoy on earth. You are heaven's ambassador. You have gained the capacity to negotiate at diplomatic level on heaven's behalf.

You, by the reason of your gained status, can now bind on earth what heaven wants bound and it shall be so. Bind the demons and bring an end to the curses they watch over to perpetuate. You can also lose on earth what heaven wants loosed. Your presence, words and actions create platforms for angelic activities. They are the ones that watch over us to actualize and perpetuate God's blessing on our behalf here on earth.

Religion and the world will often conspire in evil to rob you of your shine in Christ. They will make it look virtuous to be beaten battered and broken. They make it look like it glorifies God when you are beaten and whipped back from the market place of life by darkness. That surely is not the will of the God who called light out of darkness and loosed His son from the pain of death, and suffered none of his bone from being broken, having allowed him to go through all of the agonies for your sake. In case you are in doubt, below is the expectation of heaven concerning you in making the pain of Jesus count as gain:

> *He shall see of the travail of his soul, and shall be satisfied: by his knowledge shall my righteous servant justify many; for he shall bear their iniquities. Therefore will I divide him a portion with the great, and he shall*

> *divide the spoil with the strong. Isaiah 53:11-12a.*

There are spoils or gains of Christ's expeditions to be divided, and nothing must be strong enough to deny you your own portion of the dividend.

Make it Count for Yourself

The concept of gain from pain was designed in wisdom as a mystery by heaven and packaged for your glory. It was prototyped and showcased in Christ Jesus and now serves as the proven template of heaven for you to shine with.

> *Howbeit we speak wisdom among them that are perfect: yet not the wisdom of this world, nor of the princes of this world, that come to nought. But we speak the wisdom of God in a mystery, even the hidden wisdom, which God ordained before the world unto our glory; which none of the princes of this world knew: for had they known it, they would not have crucified the Lord of glory. 1 Corinthians 2:6-8.*

You have come out of the fall and the attending death with the curses. You have now gained life and the blessings. Applying your gain to every area of your life is a whole work on its own to be taken serious. This involves discovering what the gains are on a daily basis from the word of God. 2 Peter1:3-5. With discoveries *(revelations)* comes faith for receiving and enforcing the gains. In discoveries are terms and conditions which you have to line up with.

You need to line up your heart and mouth with gain. You need to live the gain as a lifestyle whether they are showing yet or not, till they start prevailing in your life over your present circumstance. A total re-wiring of your soul that your outlook of life may line up with the gains is a must. Romans 12:1-3.

- ***No more limitations*** - You have gained strides against and over every human limitation when it comes to living and finding fulfilment. You must not come under the ceiling again. Stay under the open heaven wherein Christ had made you sit.

- ***You are now in charge*** - You have gained power and position over and against oppression, affliction, possession and obsessions by the devil. Do not let go of you liberty because you had a bad dream or someone saw a terrible vision about you. Your positional advantage against Satan is a gain you must never compromise. Psalm 49:20. Do not relinquish your command to the enemy because of your circumstance, you are still in charge.

-        *Heaven is now ready to help* - You have gained help from on high and you must make it count. Heaven wants to really help you succeed on earth. In fact God wants you to come boldly in your present status of gain to obtain mercy and find grace in times of need. Hebrews 4:14-16

.

Make It Count For the World

> *Defend the poor and fatherless: do justice to the afflicted and needy. Deliver the poor and needy: rid them out of the hand of the wicked. They know not, neither will they understand; they walk on in darkness: all the foundations of the earth are out of course. I have said, ye are gods; and all of you are children of the most High. Psalm 82: 3-6.*

The destiny of the world is not in the hands of politicians or pressure groups as we were erroneously made to believe. The destiny of the earth is in the hands of the believers. When God wants to save all, he sends one. We are the ones sent to help the world out. There are two dimensions to our mission: we are to bring heaven to the earth and we are to lead the earth to heaven. The earth is a mid-point between hell and heaven with either side having their emissaries on earth to prevail in missions. Hell has furry and nothing good to offer; believers cannot afford to be petty, in-fighting or indifferent. We are to insist on and show justice.

We are to help the needy and be the voice for the oppressed. Truly we are not of this world, but we cannot fold our hands and let Satan make the world uninhabitable for us as if we are on a cowardly mission to quickly go hide in heaven. We need to pull our weight in the scheme of things through deep spiritual and physical endeavours. It is high time for the body of believers in Christ to stop playing the victim as if our strength is limited to number. The world needs to be saved from its sick self. It is a sick world that is resisting treatment but must be treated and healed by all and every means. If we coalesce our individual gains to form a formidable force of light, it will help us a great deal. Our gain from the pain of the master must not just be walled in within the church while the world is so in need of same.

Go out now,
Actualise your gain
Show the gain
Share the gain
Jesus is Lord.

9 780956 826749